# THE LITTLE BOOK OF
# MARY

# THE LITTLE BOOK OF
# MARY

Christine Barrely

CHRONICLE BOOKS

SAN FRANCISCO

First published in the United States of America
in 2014 by Chronicle Books LLC.
First published in France in 2012 by
Éditions du Chêne—Hachette Livre
as *Le Petit Livre de Marie*.

Library of Congress Cataloging-in-Publication Data available.

ISBN 978-1-4521-3107-8

Manufactured in China

Designed by Dinah Fried
Translated by Deborah Bruce and Elizabeth Bell

All reproductions in this book are from the private collection of
Éditions du Chêne, except images on pages 15, 21, 25, 37, 85,
and 157 © Fototeca/Leemage.

10 9 8 7 6 5 4 3 2 1

Chronicle Books LLC
680 Second Street
San Francisco, California 94107
www.chroniclebooks.com

# CONTENTS

# PREFACE

Mary is venerated in different ways by Catholic and Orthodox faithful and she is respected by Protestants as the Virgin who gave birth to Christ; she is recognized in Islam as the miraculous mother of a great prophet. She is simply a historical woman in Judaism, which does not consider her son the awaited Messiah. Mary has gathered countless devotions and legends through the centuries. She has appeared to thousands of believers throughout the world, and her devotees attribute diverse miracles and powers to her. She has inspired artists, poets, and musicians.

The evangelists, however, gave scant details of her life and personality. But the mystery of the birth of her son and the unconquerable hope born with the beginning of the Christian faith inspired a number of apocryphal texts. Not accepted in the canon of sacred literature, they are nonetheless rich in anecdotal details that have fed the beliefs of followers. Devotion to Mary in early Christian times quickly fused with the cultic honors offered to the female divinities of classical antiquity. Drawing from ancient traditions, popular rites, the dogma of the Catholic and Orthodox churches, and accounts of apparitions or strange phenomena, the life and the cult of Mary today provide an essential glimpse into Christian culture in the world.

# A VIRGIN WILL BRING FORTH
# A SAVIOR

When the story of Mary begins, Palestine had been in the hands of the Roman Empire for several decades. The Roman general and statesman Pompey had besieged Jerusalem in 63 BCE and desecrated the Temple. For more than five centuries, the Jewish people had known occupation by powerful neighbors, but they remained loyal to their cultural heritage and spiritual traditions. Some urged insurrection; all awaited a liberating savior. The Old Testament prophets were as important as ever; their visions punctuated the history of Israel.

The prophets had predicted the decline and fall of Jerusalem and exile in foreign lands. They had foreseen defeats and victories, natural catastrophes, births, and deaths. They were, at times, the only voices of hope, telling of the coming of a mysterious savior who would lead the people of Israel and restore the Kingdom of God. The birth of this messiah would itself be miraculous. Isaiah said, "Behold, a virgin shall conceive, and bear a son, and shall call his name Emmanuel." (Isaiah 7:14) The prophet Micah foretold the location of the Nativity: "But thou, Bethlehem, Ephratah, though thou be little among the thousands of Judah, yet out of thee shall come forth unto me that is to be ruler in Israel." (Micah 5:2)

CONSOLATRIX AFFLICTORUM ORA PRO NOBIS

# ANNE, THE MOTHER OF MARY

The Gospels do not tell us the name of Anne, the mother of Mary—we know it thanks to apocryphal texts. These tell that after believing herself to be sterile for twenty years, Anne gave birth to Mary. The texts also say that when Anne's aged husband Joachim died, Anne remarried and was widowed again. She married a third time; from these latter two unions were born two daughters, Mary Salome and Mary Jacob. Each of these would go on to give birth to sons who would become apostles or disciples of their cousin Jesus: John the Evangelist, James, Judas, Simon, and James the Less. Anne's daughters and grandchildren would thus play a major role in early Christianity in Palestine.

Elsewhere, veneration of Anne would take on different facets. In the sixth century, a church was dedicated to her in Constantinople, followed by other churches built in her honor. Her iconography includes scenes of her teaching Mary to read. In distant Brittany on the coast of France, one finds Anne's most fervent devotees, the earliest of whom closely linked her to the tradition of the Celtic goddess Dana. The Bretons chose Anne as patron saint and began pilgrimages, such as the ones to Sainte-Anne-d'Auray and Sainte-Anne-la-Palud. According to Breton legend, Anne was born in Brittany and only went to Palestine to give birth to Mary, finishing her days in her native land near the sea.

Sancta Anna.

# THE BIRTH OF MARY

The Gospels tell little about the life of Mary. Texts from the second century offer traditional accounts to shed light on her birth and childhood; the most informative, the apocryphal Protoevangelium of James, describes Mary's parents. Here one learns that Anne and Joachim had not conceived a child during twenty years of marriage. In despair, Joachim challenged God, saying that he would leave and stay away until Anne gave him his desired heir. At the end of forty days, an angel appeared to Joachim and told him to return to his wife. Nine months later, Anne gave birth to a girl and named her Mary, as the angel had instructed. Overwhelmed with joy, the couple vowed to consecrate their child in the Temple. When Mary was three, her parents fulfilled their promise and brought her to Jerusalem to present her to the high priest.

According to James, Mary grew up in Galilee in the town of Nazareth. Her parents honored the Jewish holy days and taught their child the words of the prophets. Mary grew from a tenderly nurtured child to a sweet and hardworking adolescent. Her family sought a good husband for her when she was twelve, the age for betrothal in that era. For Mary, the choice fell on Joseph, a carpenter of good reputation. After their term of engagement, Mary and Joseph were wed.

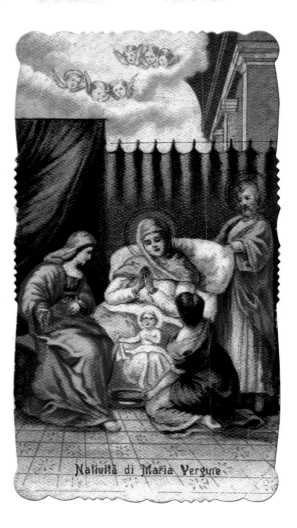

Natività di Maria Vergine

# THE ANNUNCIATION

The Annunciation, described in the Gospel of Luke, took place in the humble agricultural town of Nazareth in Galilee. Mary had been recently betrothed to Joseph. Like her, the carpenter was a distant descendent of David, the celebrated king of Israel. According to custom, Mary still lived with her parents until the time that her marriage would be consecrated.

One day, a stranger appeared to Mary and told her that she had been chosen among all women. She was disconcerted and somewhat frightened, but the stranger, the archangel Gabriel, reassured her with the words, "Fear not, Mary, for thou hast found favor with God." (Luke 1:30) Then Gabriel told her that she would conceive a child and would give birth to a son to be named Jesus, meaning "Savior." The angel said that the child would inherit the throne of David and reign forever. Mary doubted the angel's message, knowing herself to be a virgin. Gabriel told her that the Holy Spirit would descend on her and that God would miraculously impregnate her while she would still remain a virgin. "For this reason the child to be born will be called the Son of God," the angel concluded. But when Mary told Joseph what had happened, he was overwhelmed and wanted to end their betrothal. Only when an angel appeared to him in a dream and told him that the pregnancy came from God, was Joseph persuaded to go on with the marriage.

Dixit autem Maria: Ecce ancilla Domini, fiat mihi secundum verbum tuum. Luc. l. 38.

Société de St Augustin.

*And Mary said, Behold the handmaid of the Lord; be it unto me according to thy word.* LUKE 1:38

# JOSEPH, THE HUSBAND OF MARY

Who was this man who agreed, in highly patriarchal times, to marry a young bride who was already pregnant? Undoubtedly, he must have had deep faith to believe what the angel told him about the supernatural pregnancy of his betrothed, and certainly had great love to take in this young woman and accept that she remained a virgin. Joseph fulfilled the role of legal father for the young Jesus, and was a loyal husband to Mary. The Gospels describe a good man, pious and just, with a strong sense of responsibility. We know that he was a carpenter and that he taught his trade to the young Jesus, who worked at his side.

As with Mary, apocryphal texts tell us more about Joseph, such as that he was much older than Mary, he was a widower at the time of their betrothal, and he was already a father from his earlier marriage. The circumstances of his death are not to be found, but we know that Joseph died before Jesus, since when Mary is mentioned in the Gospels at the Marriage at Cana and at the foot of the Cross, Joseph is not present. Thus Jesus, before breathing his last, would entrust the care of his mother to his disciple John.

# THE VISITATION

After Gabriel revealed to Mary that she would bear a son, the archangel told her of another miracle, that her cousin Elisabeth, aged and barren, had also become pregnant. Before this time, Elisabeth and her husband Zacharias had hoped in vain for a child, but had resigned themselves to remaining childless. Gabriel told Mary that Elisabeth was already six months pregnant. Mary then left for the hills of Judea to visit her cousin. At Elisabeth's door, Mary warmly embraced her, and in that instant the child that Mary carried in her womb moved with such strength that Elisabeth, feeling the Holy Spirit, realized that Mary's baby was not an ordinary child and that he was truly sent by God. Mary expressed her gratitude to the Lord, knowing that God had elected her to give birth to the Savior.

The two women of such different ages felt profoundly linked by the miraculous nature of their pregnancies and by the certainty of being chosen by God. Mary stayed for three months with her cousin, then returned to Galilee to prepare for the birth of her own child. Elisabeth gave birth to a son, whom she named John. Her son grew up to preach the coming of the Messiah and came to be known as John the Baptist, he who would baptize his cousin Jesus.

*Visita della Santissima Vergine
a Santa Elisabetta.*

DÉPOSÉ

Tipografia S. Lega Eucaristica.

# THE NATIVITY

The evangelists Matthew and Luke recount that Joseph took Mary as his wife, accepting that she was a virgin. Shortly before the time for Mary to give birth, the Roman emperor Caesar Augustus ordered a census to tax all the inhabitants in the empire. All were to return to their hometown to be counted. Joseph was from Bethlehem in Judea, so the couple departed from Nazareth, Mary riding on a donkey led by her husband. The journey was nearly a hundred miles and took many days. When they reached Bethlehem, they found the town crowded with travelers who had come for the same reason. Joseph and Mary went from inn to inn, but could find nowhere to stay. Night was falling, so Joseph made a place for his wife in a humble stable, perhaps a cave used to shelter animals, such as were common in the hills around the town.

Exhausted by the journey, Mary felt the onset of her labor. Joseph made a simple bed of straw, where Mary brought forth her child into the world, alone, without the customary help of older women. She wrapped her baby in swaddling clothes, using a manger—the animals' feeding trough—for his cradle. The miraculous child foretold by the angel Gabriel was born, and he was named Jesus.

Je ne suis pas venu pour
juger, mais pour sauver...
℣ Je ne veux pas la mort
du pécheur, mais qu'il se
convertisse, et qu'il vive.

*I have come not to judge but to save . . . I wish not for the sinner to die, but that
he may convert and live.*

# THE ADORATION
# OF THE SHEPHERDS

Of all the scenes of the lives of Mary and Jesus, the Adoration of the Shepherds is among the most popular. The Gospel of Luke tells that at the time of the Nativity, the shepherds near Bethlehem stayed through the night with their flocks in the hills. An angel appeared to them with a dazzling brightness, and said, "Fear not, behold, I bring you good tidings of great joy, which shall be to all people. For unto you is born this day in the city of David a Savior . . ." and a multitude of angels appeared, singing, "Glory to God in the highest, and on earth peace, good will toward men." The shepherds hastened into Bethlehem and found the stable, where they saw Mary, Joseph, and the child, and they knelt in adoration.

The scene is familiar from the tradition of the Christmas crèche. The celebration of Christmas began in the fourth century; the use of a crèche scene to commemorate the Nativity began one or two centuries later. The Jesuits continued the tradition in the sixteenth century. According to custom, the scene includes Mary, Joseph, the donkey that came with them to Nazareth, and an ox whose breath warmed the infant. To symbolize the birth, the figure of the newborn is not added until the night of December twenty-fourth. The shepherds and a few sheep complete the scene. A star is often added atop the crèche, recalling the one that guided the Magi to the newborn Christ.

Gloria in excelsis Deo

# THE COMING OF THE MAGI

The adoration of the Holy Child by the Magi is described in only one of the Gospels, by the evangelist Matthew, and in apocryphal texts. The Three Kings, the priestly Wise Men from the East, had been told in dreams to follow a bright star that would lead them to the new king of the Jews. They gathered precious offerings for the child and went on their journey in search of the new king. Herod, the current king of Israel, learned of their approach and sought to know their purpose. When the Magi reached Jerusalem, Herod sent them on to Bethlehem, where the Prophets had foretold the birth of the Savior. Herod, fearing a rival, told the Magi to return to tell him what they found. Guided by the star, the Magi found the stable, where they presented their gifts of gold, frankincense, and myrrh for Jesus and his mother, Mary. That night, in a dream, they were warned to not return to Herod and to take a different route home. Scripture tells no more about these men, but later Armenian accounts describe them as three great men of diverse race and color, named Caspar, Melchior, and Balthasar.

Figures of the Magi are traditionally placed in the Christmas crèche along with Jesus, Mary, and Joseph, but the actual celebration of the visit of the Wise Men is on the sixth of January, the feast of Epiphany, commemorating the manifestation of Christ to the Gentiles. On this day, some cultures still exchange gifts.

Les Mages ouvrant leurs trésors offrirent
au Seigneur de l'or,
de l'encens et de la myrrhe.
*(St. Matthieu, II, 11.)*

Boumard Fils, Paris.                                          5344

*When the Magi opened their treasures, they presented unto the Lord gold,*
*frankincense and myrrh.* MATTHEW 2:11

# THE FLIGHT INTO EGYPT

After his account of the visit of the Magi, the evangelist Matthew tells of a sudden turn of events that we know of as the Massacre of the Innocents. King Herod, furious that the Magi did not return to report to him, and jealous of the acclaim given to this unknown newborn, ordered the massacre of all the boys under the age of two in Bethlehem and the rest of Judea. Fortunately Joseph, the husband of Mary, had dreamt that an angel told him to take Mary and Jesus away to Egypt. Joseph left without delay for the land south of Palestine, traveling with a donkey for his wife and child.

Herod believed he had fulfilled his sinister decree, having savagely killed many young innocents. Joseph kept his family in the land of the pharaohs and lived there quietly for several years, until the death of King Herod. An angel then came again to Joseph to tell him he could return to his country. Out of caution, Joseph did not return to Bethlehem but settled in Galilee, in the town of Nazareth. This narrative has been a common subject in Christian art since the Middle Ages, notably in sculptures on Romanesque churches and in paintings by Fra Angelico, Carpaccio, and later, Poussin.

# MARY AND THE
# CHILDHOOD OF JESUS

Little is revealed in the Gospels about Mary's life during the childhood of Jesus. Joseph and Mary had their son circumcised when he was eight days old, and presented him in the Temple for his ritual purification. Jesus grew up quietly with his parents, their years following the cycles of the Jewish holy days. Mary concerned herself with raising her son, teaching him respect for the Sabbath and other religious traditions. A respected carpenter, Joseph no doubt kept busy in his workshop. Jesus learned the sacred texts and knew the history of the chosen people.

When Jesus was twelve, the family went—as they did every year—to Jerusalem for Passover. As they started the journey home at the end of the festival, Mary and Joseph realized that Jesus was not among the kinsmen who traveled with them. They searched for three days without finding him until they returned to the Temple, where Jesus sat in debate over the scriptures with the doctors of the law. Mary reproached him for having worried them so. Although Jesus greatly respected his mother, his retort to her was that he had to tend to his Father's concerns. Mary and Joseph did not understand what he meant with these words. For the first time, Jesus had expressed to them that his spiritual relationship would be of the highest importance.

Et il leur était soumis. (Luc, II, 51.)

Société St. Augustin, Bruges, A. h. 73.

*And he was obedient to them.* LUKE 2:51

# THE SUFFERINGS OF MARY

The Gospels relate the first part of Mary's life as a series of blessings and happy moments, but her role as a mother became more complex once her son was baptized and embarked on his ministry. Jesus left home and began to preach and gather new disciples. Mary saw him less, but she was present to witness his first miracle, when he transformed water to wine at the Marriage at Cana. Widowed, Mary followed her son for some of his travels, convinced by his message. But as a mother, she worried about her son, who gave ever more of himself while his critics multiplied.

Jesus often reminded his mother that those who believed in him had become his true family, and he also told her that he was destined to suffer and to be killed. These words made Mary love her son all the more. She would see him for the last time when she went to Jerusalem for Passover when Jesus was thirty-three years old. He had been condemned to death; one imagines her, waiting before the palace of Pontius Pilate for confirmation of the decree, then following the appalling procession to Golgotha as her son endured horrendous tortures. We see her grieving at the foot of the Cross, pierced with sorrow when her son dies, is taken from the Cross, and is carried to the sepulcher.

Sotto la croce

N. D. des sept douleurs. ✢ ✢ ✢ Bajo la cruz

Unter dem Kreuze. Beneath the Cross.

# MARY AT PENTECOST

The scriptures attest that Mary kept her faith in her son's teachings after the Crucifixion, strengthened by her witness to the miracles that surrounded his death. Before Jesus drew his last breath, total darkness overtook the sun. It is written that at the moment of his death, the veil at the inner sanctuary of the Temple tore apart and a great earthquake shook. After the Resurrection of Jesus on the third day after he died, he was seen by his followers over the course of forty days. During this time, he told them to wait in Jerusalem, saying that they were to be baptized in the Holy Spirit, which would descend upon them, and they would become his witnesses to the far ends of the earth.

Mary and the other women who had accompanied Jesus would meet, along with the other disciples, at a house in Jerusalem. Fifty days after Passover, on the Jewish festival of Shabuoth or Pentecost, they were there when they heard a sound from the sky like the rushing of a mighty wind and saw tongues of fire appear upon each other's heads. Filled with the Holy Spirit, they began to speak in many languages—to the bewilderment and amazement of the people who had gathered outside the house after hearing the roaring wind. Among them were foreigners who could hear in their own languages the teachings of God. The apostle Peter proclaimed, "God has made this same Jesus, whom you crucified, both Lord and Messiah." (Acts 2:36)

# La Pentecôte.

Et repleti sunt omnes Spiritu Sancto. Act II 4.

Société de St Augustin

*And they were all filled with the Holy Spirit.* ACTS 2:4

# THE DORMITION AND ASSUMPTION

The Dormition refers to the passing of Mary from earthly life, not described in the Gospels but recorded in a sixth-century text attributed to a writer referred to as pseudo-John. This narrative tells that Mary returned faithfully to the empty burial place of her son. On a Friday, the angel Gabriel came to her and told her that she would soon rise to heaven to find her son again. Mary decided to go to Bethlehem, and prayed that John and the other apostles would be beside her. The Holy Spirit brought John from Ephesus, Peter from Rome, Paul from the banks of the Tiber, and Thomas from India. They all found themselves reunited around Mary. As they prayed, they heard the sound of thunder, a host of angels appeared, and a loud voice came from the sky. The narrative says that the Holy Spirit transported Mary and the apostles back to Jerusalem, where on Sunday, while angels surrounded her house, Jesus called to her from heaven. She died, and the apostles took her body to a tomb in the Garden of Gethsemane. On the third day, angels came to carry her body to paradise.

The celebration of the holy day or feast of the Assumption is on the fifteenth of August. The Orthodox Church observes this date as the feast of the Dormition. The Roman Catholic Church declared the dogma of the Assumption, that Mary was assumed—taken to heaven without actually dying or being buried—only in 1950.

# VENERATION OF MARY

Readings of the four Gospels and the Acts of the Apostles give little indication that Mary received special veneration in the faith of the earliest Christians. Second-century texts refer to Christ as "Son of God, born of Mary." Around the year 165 CE, Saint Justin the Martyr was the first to put in writing the phrase of "the Virgin" in reference to Mary. Early in the third century, increasing reverence for her was expressed with prayers. Her cult of veneration grew in the next century, especially in the Eastern Church. In the early fifth century, a debate raged as to whether she could be called the Mother of God. The Council of Ephesus settled the matter in 431, and the feast day of Mary, Mother of God, the first of January, was established.

Veneration of Mary took on great importance in the Middle Ages. Chapels, abbeys, and cathedrals were dedicated to her. Important figures in the Church through the centuries have affirmed their devotion to her, such as Bernard of Clairvaux, Saint Teresa of Avila, and Saint John of the Cross. In the Orthodox Church, Mary is likewise venerated, but without reference to the dogmas of the Immaculate Conception (that she herself was conceived without original sin) or her Assumption to heaven. Protestant believers accept as an article of faith the Gospel accounts of the Virgin Birth, but do not practice the special devotions offered to Mary by Catholic and Orthodox faithful.

*Offrande de St. Louis de Gonzaque à la bienheureuse Vierge Marie.*

Offering of St. Aloysius Gonzaga to the blessèd Virgin Mary.

# THE IMMACULATE CONCEPTION

Among the teachings of the Catholic Church, the dogma of the Immaculate Conception of Mary was confirmed late, not until 1854. It conveys the idea that God freed Mary from original sin; that she was conceived as a pure being with no propensity for evil. When Pope Pius IX declared the belief as official dogma, he put an end to centuries of theological debate. Two opposing theories had competed since the twelfth century. Thomas Aquinas and Bernard of Clairvaux asserted that only Christ had been born free of the sinful state of the human soul; Mary, because she was born before Christ, would therefore have been born capable of sin like anyone. Opposing this view, other theologians claimed that Mary was conceived free from original sin. Thus she was born in a special state of grace that set her apart from the rest of humanity, a grace without which she could not have brought Jesus into the world.

The Council of Basle (1431–49) and especially the Council of Trent (1546) reinforced this teaching. In 1708, the pope established the feast of the Immaculate Conception on the eighth of December, the same date as the feast of the Nativity of Mary. The Orthodox Church dismisses the Immaculate Conception, and Protestant denominations firmly reject it. In iconography, the Virgin of the Immaculate Conception stands with outspread arms or with her hands clasped in prayer, with downcast eyes or looking up.

LA VIERGE IMMACULÉE.

# A FIRST COMMUNION SOUVENIR

In recognition of the importance of the veneration of Mary, images illustrating scenes of her life have been customary gifts at the time of a young person's First Communion. The motherly qualities of the Virgin evoked protection for the child as well as Mary's role as intercessor conveying prayers to her son. Mary might be depicted receiving Communion or accompanying children at their First Communion.

The tradition of holy images was popularized in the nineteenth century with the modernization of printing, first in the form of illustrations in small prayer books or missals. These small books became a favored gift at First Communions. Pious images were also distributed as individual "holy cards," as an aid to the faithful for prayer and meditation. Produced in abundance and great variety, sometimes printed with prayers, holy cards would be given at the rite of Confirmation as well as First Communion. The choice of iconography served an educational purpose, as the images reflected teachings of the Catholic faith and were offered at the time of the ritual marking the end of catechism or spiritual apprenticeship and entry into the age of adult belief.

Gedenkenis
der H. Communie.

DÉPOSÉ

# MARIAN BLUE

Mary's emblematic color has been blue since the art of the eleventh and twelfth centuries. Earlier—with the exception of the Egyptians, who associated blue with the afterlife—the ancient world gave greatest value to red and purple, symbols of wealth and power. Advances in textile dyeing techniques permitted the use of pigments and dyes that could create vivid and lightfast blues. Cool and deep as the sky, blue soon overtook the use of reds and yellows. The Roman Church chose blue to depict Mary's robes, departing from traditional Byzantine reds. Along with virginal white—the absence of color—a sky blue or "Marian blue" symbolizes Mary's proximity to God and her purity and transcendence. It is also associated with the spiritual and the immaterial in Aztec, Hindu, Buddhist, and other cultures.

In the twelfth century, the king of France himself renounced the color red for his cloak and adopted blue. Gothic art in the Middle Ages made abundant use of this color, along with gold, to depict the sun and light associated with the divine. In the Renaissance, the blue used to paint the Virgin became lighter and clearer, a fitting hue for the image of tenderness more and more sought by artists. In devotional imagery, the blue or white robe symbolizing Mary's purity is sometimes enhanced with a red tunic to evoke the blood shed by Christ.

Marie est la mère de l'Espérance : elle fait paître dans nos cœurs l'espoir de la grâce de Dieu, du vrai bonheur, et de la félicité éternelle.

St Bernard

BOUASSE JEUNE, PARIS. 1011

*Mary is the mother of Hope: she engenders in our hearts the hope of God's grace, true happiness, and eternal joy.*

# QUEEN OF ANGELS

"Queen of Angels, pray for us." Among the invocations of the Virgin, this prayer makes direct reference to Mary's supremacy among the angels. Another prayer sung to Mary, the celebrated hymn *Salve Regina (Hail, [Holy] Queen)* also begins with a salutation to Mary as a queen. These examples from the twelfth and thirteenth centuries attest to the high status given to Mary in the Middle Ages. Thomas Aquinas emphasized that the salutation of the archangel to Mary at the Annunciation was imbued with reverence. Apocryphal texts describe the events of the Dormition and Assumption of the Virgin as occurring in the presence of clouds of angels who bowed before the Virgin Mary. The Gospels give little indication of such phenomena other than the Annunciation; nonetheless, the Catholic Church dubs Mary the Queen of Angels.

The iconography of the Virgin often includes one or two figures of angels; for the Assumption, a multitude of angels gathers around her. Many churches are dedicated to Mary of the Angels or Our Lady of the Angels, such as in Rome and Assisi, or, more modestly, at Collioure, France.

Montrez que vous êtes notre mère, et qu'il reçoive par vous nos prières, Celui qui, né pour nous, voulut être votre Fils.

*Make manifest that you are our mother, and through you may our prayers reach the One who, born for us, chose to be your Son.*

# MARY CROWNED WITH STARS

The Apocalypse or Book of Revelation, a book of scripture full of symbolism, provides the most majestic image of Mary. The vision of end times does not name Mary but describes "a woman clothed with the sun, and the moon under her feet, and upon her head a crown of twelve stars: And she being with child cried, travailing in birth, and pained to be delivered." (Apocalypse 12:1) The narrative then tells of a great dragon the color of fire, who waits to devour the newborn. The nameless woman gives birth to a son. This child, who is to rule the world, is taken to God's side. Angels then cast the dragon out of heaven to the earth. There the dragon, none other than the devil, pursues the woman. She has been given wings that allow her to escape into the wilderness.

The Catholic Church borrowed this imagery from Revelation to represent the Virgin Mary in resplendent robes, standing atop the moon and crushing a dragon underfoot. The crown symbolizes her victory over evil and her immortality; the twelve stars are said to symbolize the twelve tribes of Israel, to signify a great assemblage of humankind.

Regina sine labe originali concepta
ora pro nobis

Queen conceived without original sin, pray for us.

# STABAT MATER

*Stabat Mater* is the name of the celebrated thirteenth-century hymn that recounts the sufferings of the Virgin Mary. Composed in Latin by the Franciscan monk Jacopone da Todi in Italy, it begins with these words: "Stabat mater dolorosa, juxta crucem lacrimosa." (The mother stands full of sorrow, in tears beside the Cross.) The work is a long meditation that invites one to share the sorrow of a woman who sees her son perish in terrible agony: "O quam tristis et afflicta fuit illa benedicta, mater unigeniti!" (How sad and distressed was the blessèd mother of the only-begotten One!)

One of several hymns evoking the grieving Mary, the popularity of the *Stabat Mater* grew along with the rise in devotion to the Virgin. Through the centuries, composers who have set the words to music include Pergolesi, Scarlatti, Vivaldi, Haydn, Schubert, and Verdi. In the liturgy, the *Stabat Mater* is associated with the feast of Our Lady of Sorrows on the fifteenth of September, the day after Holy Cross Day (the feast of the Exaltation of the Cross), on the fourteenth of September.

QVAM
TRISTIS
ET·AFFLICTA
FVIT·ILLA·
BENEDICTA
MATER @
VNIGENITI (Stab. Mat.)

M. Lemaire, 10.                    Made in Belgium.

*How sad and distressed was the blessèd mother of the only-begotten One.*

# THE ROSARY

Devotion to Mary is often practiced as a meditation by long recitation of prayers while "telling" or counting the beads of a rosary. This custom dates from the Middle Ages, although ritualized use of strands of beads existed since ancient times in diverse cultures. A tradition recounts that Saint Dominic received the first rosary beads from the Virgin herself; it was within the Dominican Order that use of the rosary first became widespread.

Guiding recitation of the rosary prayers, the faithful use a string of beads made up of five groups of ten beads separated by larger beads. Attached to one section are three smaller beads plus a larger one, and a crucifix. For each bead in a group of ten, one says a Hail Mary, and for each large bead, an Our Father; reaching the crucifix, one recites the Credo. Five times in telling the rosary, these devotions involve meditation on the mysteries—episodes in the lives of the Virgin and Christ. The mysteries include five that are joyous, such as the Annunciation and the Nativity; five that are sorrowful, such as the Flagellation and the Crucifixion; and five glorious mysteries, including the Ascension of Christ and the Coronation of Mary in heaven. The Catholic Church has consecrated the month of October to the rosary since 1887.

REGINA

SACRATISSIMI ROSARII

ORA PRO NOBIS.

*Queen of the most sacred rosary, pray for us.*

# THE MYSTICAL ROSE

"Mystical Rose, pray for us"—litanies dedicated to the Virgin composed in the sixteenth century were not the first to use this name; in the Middle Ages, Saint Bernard compared Mary to a rose without thorns, a "mystical rose." Considered the queen of flowers, the rose was associated in ancient times with deities such as the Greek goddess Aphrodite or the Roman goddess Venus. Among the early Christians, the rose evoked paradise; it became an emblem of the Virgin by the beginning of the fifth century. The idea of the thornless rose made direct reference to the Immaculate Conception, the dogma that states that Mary was born without original sin. The most beautiful flower echoed the most saintly of women.

We find the rose in images of the Virgin in Orthodox as well as Roman Catholic iconography. Like the lily, the other Marian flower, the rose symbolizes the absolute love that the Virgin has for her celestial "bridegroom." Woven into a crown or strewn as a carpet before her, roses adorn processions in her honor or decorate statues of the Virgin. The telling of the beads of the rosary has been compared to plucking the petals of a flower. In religious imagery, the rose is the attribute of Mary as well as Jesus and numerous saints.

MATER PURISSIMA

*Ora Pro Nobis*

# AVE MARIA

With the Pater Noster (the Our Father), the Ave Maria (Hail Mary) is the most frequently recited prayer among Catholics. It recalls the words of the archangel Gabriel when he told Mary she would miraculously carry the son of God—in Latin, *Ave Maria, gratia plena* (Hail Mary, full of grace)—as well as the words of Elisabeth when Mary came to visit her. This first part of the prayer is an invocation that reprises a detail of the Gospel of Luke. Recited since the fourth or fifth century in the Orthodox Church as well as by Roman Catholics, it became widespread in the Middle Ages, especially among monastics of the Dominican Order.

The second part of the prayer, which refers to Mary, Mother of God, was added to the Catholic liturgy in the sixteenth century. It is a supplication for the intercession of the Virgin. When the Hail Mary is recited as part of the rosary prayer, it is said in five series of ten repetitions. Long chanted by the faithful, this prayer has inspired many musicians—the *Ave Marias* of Schubert, Gounod, and Bach are among the most beautiful compositions of sacred music.

Abe, Maria, gratia plena: Dominus tecum: benedicta tu in mulieribus, et benedictus fructus bentris tui, Jesus. Sancta Maria, Mater Dei, ora pro nobis peccatoribus, nunc et in hora mortis nostræ. Amen.

AVE MARIA

L. TURGIS & FILS.    70    EDIT. IMP. PARIS

*Hail Mary, full of grace, the Lord is with thee; blessèd art thou amongst women, and blessèd is the fruit of thy womb, Jesus. Holy Mary, mother of God, pray for us sinners, now and in the hour of our death. Amen.*

# MAY, THE MONTH OF MARY

The tradition of honoring Mary in the month of May originated in Italy in the thirteenth century, first in Rome, later reaching Naples and Sicily. In the sixteenth century, Saint Filippo Neri, founder of the Fathers of the Oratory, started a May celebration for children in honor of Mary. The tradition spread under the auspices of the Jesuits, who very actively promoted the cult of the Virgin during the Counter-Reformation. In churches, altarpieces accentuating the importance of Mary became numerous, painted or sculpted with depictions of scenes from the life of the Virgin.

The month of May, the time of the renewal of nature and her surge of flowers—coming after the feast of Easter, the celebration of the Resurrection of Christ— was designated by papal decree as a month for Marian devotion in 1815, calling for daily prayers to honor Mary as well as other honors and good works. Small prayer books were printed for these observances, and families were encouraged to read from them each day in the presence of an image of the Virgin.

Mère Admirable.

Mater Admirabilis

# THE PATRONESS OF FRANCE

In the seventeenth century, Louis XIII, the king of France, was moved to dedicate his kingdom to the Virgin Mary. She had appeared to a monk and foretold the birth of an heir, the future Louis XIV, after twenty-two years of childlessness for the king and the queen, Anne of Austria. On the tenth of February 1638, the king solemnly proclaimed "the vow of Louis XIII": "We declare that, taking the very holy and very glorious Virgin as special protectress of our kingdom, we consecrate to her our person, our State, our crown, and our subjects, beseeching her to inspire in ourselves holy conduct, and to defend with great care this kingdom against all our enemies, so that, whether it suffers the scourge of war or enjoys the sweetness of peace, it never leaves the ways of grace that lead to those of glory."

This expression of gratitude to the Virgin, which made her the patroness and protector of France, was accompanied by a vow to construct a great altar in the cathedral of Notre-Dame de Paris, to be adorned with a figure of the Virgin at the foot of the Cross, holding the dead Christ in her arms. Louis XIII died before fulfilling this promise, but his son, Louis XIV, saw the monument completed in 1714.

Reine
des Martyrs,
priez pour nous.

Dep<sup>t</sup> 4221 F

Queen of martyrs, pray for us.

# MIRACULOUS VIRGINS

The making of carved or painted images to give tangible form to the belief of the faithful was established in the Roman Church by the eighth century, and the cult of relics and holy images used as objects of reverence spread throughout Christendom in the Middle Ages. Regarding devotion to the Virgin Mary, the belief that she was physically elevated to heaven meant that she left no relics in the form of corporeal remains. These circumstances help to explain the extraordinary devotion offered to icons of the Virgin.

Countless legends tell of miraculous images that appeared—to give victory to an army, command the construction of a shrine, or protect a village from danger. Sometimes the discovery of a statue of the Virgin, lost or hidden for decades or more, is greeted as if it were a miraculous apparition. A site of a shrine secures her patronage and invokes the protection of the statue as if it were the Virgin herself. The statue is embellished, dressed, adorned with flowers, bedecked with jewels, and carried in procession through the streets. In Spain, for example, the Virgen del Rocío in Andalusia was discovered by a shepherd who tried to bring the statue back to his village. When he came to a marsh, the oxen carrying the statue refused to go on, revealing that this was the spot where a shrine must be built. There the statue became an object of fervent pilgrimage, attracting a million worshipers at Pentecost.

O Marie Médiatrice universelle des grâces p.p.n.

Litho. Em. Lombaerts-Van de Velde, Dearne. Anvers

Mary, universal intercessor in grace, pray for us.

# CHILDREN OF
# THE IMMACULATE MARY

In the sixteenth century, in response to the Protestant Reformation, the Catholic Church launched a vast campaign for the spiritual reconquest of the faithful. With emphasis on the need for evangelization and rediscovery of the original purity of the Church, education was placed at the heart of reforms. In Paris in 1617, the French priest Vincent de Paul founded a charitable association of women called the Daughters of Charity. These laywomen devoted themselves to serving the destitute, the sick, and the homeless. In 1641, they began to teach Marian devotions to the children who they served.

In 1830, the Sisters of Charity of St. Vincent de Paul decided to offer an intensive education to selected youth from among the common people, in order to create a "pious elite" entirely devoted to the Virgin Mary. These became the Children of the Immaculate Mary. Their upbringing would be moral, but also practical, to make them useful workers in their society. Each Child of Mary would wear the "miraculous medal" of Catherine Labouré—herself a Daughter of Charity—attached to a ribbon: green for novices, sky blue for graduates, and purple for those who had married.

Fleurs des Enfants de Marie

O Vierge Marie, fleur sortie des épines, fleur sans épines, priez pour nous!

stc

F. BOUASSE Jne Edr          3475          RUE MABILLON, 9, PARIS

**ABOVE:** *Flowers of the Children of Mary*
**BELOW:** *O Virgin Mary, flower among thorns, flower without thorns, pray for us!*

# THE IMMACULATE HEART OF MARY

Feast days for the Sacred Heart of Jesus and the Immaculate Heart of Mary were celebrated in the seventeenth century, among a number of feast days advanced fairly late by the Catholic Church. A priest from Normandy, Jean Eudes, founded the Congregation of Jesus and Mary, dedicated to veneration of these two sacred hearts. Devotion to the Sacred Heart of Jesus acknowledges gratitude for the love Christ had in giving his life for humankind. The iconography shows a heart on a cross, surrounded by flames and thorns, pierced by a lance and flowing with blood. The Immaculate Heart of Mary, also called the Sacred Heart of Mary, is also depicted surrounded by flames, symbolizing love, and pierced with a sword as a sign of the sorrows borne by Mary at the time of her son's death.

In the apparitions of the Virgin at Fátima in Portugal in 1917, Mary linked the salvation of the world to devotion to her Immaculate Heart. Just after the Second World War, Pope Pius XII declared the twenty-second of August the official date for the feast day of the Immaculate Heart of Mary, one week after the feast of the Assumption—special times of veneration to honor the qualities of goodness, generosity, and purity that Mary manifests.

*Puisse, ô Marie, mon cœur*
*toujours brûler et mon âme*
*se consumer pour vous.*

S. Bouguereau.

O Mary, may my heart always burn and my soul consume itself for you.

# OUR LADY OF DELIVERANCE

Among the prayers or supplications addressed to Mary, those offered to Our Lady of Deliverance appeal to the power of the Virgin to liberate those who venerate her, be they actual prisoners or those held captive in less tangible ways. For deliverance in the sense of childbirth, the Virgin Mary's experience as a woman and a mother empower her to intercede on behalf of pregnant women, to protect them from premature or false labor or difficult childbirth. A great many churches and cathedrals are named for Our Lady of Deliverance, such as Notre-Dame-de-la-Délivrance in Quintin, Brittany, where every year on the second Sunday in May, a *pardon*—a Breton pilgrimage—is held in honor of the Virgin, when a relic considered to be a sash belonging to her is carried in procession through the town.

In the twelfth century, at the abbey of Igny in the Marne region of France, the Cistercian abbot Guerric described his own fervent prayers to the Virgin to participate in her delivery of Jesus himself. He saw the Virgin as a symbol of spiritual maternity in such a way that every believer, including himself, a monk, could take part with her in giving birth and "delivering" the infant Jesus. Thus the monk could, in a way, implant Christ in his own heart and protect this divine embryo from any false labor—"conceiving God within."

NOTRE DAME DE LA DÉLIVRANCE

# OUR LADY OF MERCY

Our Lady of Mercy, a manifestation also known as Our Lady of Protection, was an enormously popular aspect of the Virgin in the Middle Ages and through the Renaissance, known from much earlier times and depicted in Byzantine and Gothic paintings. In Italy, medieval painters created small votive panels used to invoke the protection of Our Lady of Mercy. Depicted standing, majestic, and noticeably larger than the other figures in the image, she always wears a long cloak that she opens with her arms to shelter those who entrust themselves to her. In doing so, she shows her tenderness and benevolence toward the poor, the humble, and the feeble. This is the archetype of the Virgin as one who protects and consoles. Usually the child Jesus is absent from these images, and the Virgin appears in a flat and empty pictorial space, but one richly embellished with stars or other gilded motifs. The faithful receiving her protection kneel or stand in prayer.

Besides the medieval Italian painters inspired by this theme, sculptors also carved the scene for many chapels and churches. In Seville, the remarkable altarpiece known as the *Retablo de la Casa de Contratación* shows her protecting the Spanish king and the fleet of Columbus. Images of the cloaked Virgin of Mercy appear throughout the Burgundy region of France; known as Notre-Dame de Consolation, legends attribute to them miraculous gifts of protection.

# VIRGIN AND CHILD

The first representations of the Virgin and Child are known from the third century. The oldest example was found in Rome in the catacomb of Priscilla, from the same era as early apocryphal accounts of the life of the Virgin, such as the Protoevangelium of James. The Gospels were written by the end of the first century, centered on the life of Jesus and with little detail about Mary. As the Christian religion grew, interest in Mary increased. In the first centuries of the faith, Christian thinkers professed the belief that Christ was incarnated by the Holy Spirit and the Virgin Mary. Despite little evidence of an early devotional cult for Mary, the image of this "divine maternity" grew swiftly in popular appeal, having a correspondence to ancient, pre-Christian depictions of mother goddesses and sacred virgins.

The first indications of special veneration of Mary became evident in prayers addressed to the Virgin in the third century, when she became a kind of intermediary. With time, her iconography developed accordingly. Byzantine tradition presented her in a solemn, stylized manner, seated in majesty on a throne with her child Jesus on her knees. More and more frequently in the art of the early Middle Ages, she was seen as the Virgin of Tenderness, holding the child Jesus on her knees, with her arms around him. She leaned toward him, gradually adopting a more and more natural pose.

MATER DIVINÆ GRATIÆ

Mère de la divine grâce,
priez pour nous.

BOUASSE JEUNE      1144      PARIS

Mother of divine grace, pray for us.

# MARY AND THE BIRDS

Depictions of Mary and Jesus often reflect established conventions and carry the same iconography from one image to the next. But more inventive interpretations can be found. The presence of one or more birds accompanying the Virgin and Child is a variant inspired by tradition. A legend tells of an incident in the Flight into Egypt, when Mary was injured and was bleeding. A robin followed her, hiding the drops of blood she left and thus threw off her pursuers. The little redbreast would be blessed among all the birds.

Another legend, from the apocryphal Gospel of Thomas, describes the infant Jesus forming small birds of clay and then making them come alive. Iconography often shows the saints with birds, continuing older traditions that give them symbolic significance. Artists Dürer and Raphael depicted the Virgin and Child with a goldfinch—its plumage tinged with red prefigures the Passion and Crucifixion to come. A bird may carry other symbolism. In the Gospels, the Holy Spirit materializes as a dove. Moving between earth and sky, birds evoke the world of the spirit and represent the soul.

Vierge aimable, obtenez-moi la grâce
de partager les joies de votre Fils
par la pratique de la simplicité.

MAISON BOUASSE-LEBEL — Dauverne & Cie — PARIS.  2785
MADE IN FRANCE

*Kind Virgin, grant me the grace to share your Son's joys by living a humble life.*

# THE HOLY FAMILY

Mary, Joseph, and Jesus became known to the Catholic Church as the Holy Family, serving as a model for Christian families. Since the fifteenth century, the Church made Joseph an exemplar as a foster father to Jesus and husband to Mary, and the art of the Renaissance emphasized his humanity through images of the Nativity. Veneration of Joseph spread in the sixteenth century, coinciding with the emergence of the notion of the Holy Family at the time of the Counter-Reformation. Paintings and sculptures were commissioned by the Church to bring the faithful back to the Gospels and Catholic doctrines. Images of the Holy Family became numerous, expressing the virtues of love, compassion, and filial piety. Michelangelo, Raphael, Rembrandt, Rubens, Poussin, and Murillo, among many other artists, created extraordinary examples.

The Sunday following Christmas marks the feast day of the Holy Family. Holy cards often associate the earthly trio of the Holy Family with the celestial Trinity—God the Father, the Holy Spirit (seen as a dove), and Jesus—a comparison with no actual basis in scripture.

La sacra famiglia.

La sainte famille. ✢ ✢ La sagrada familia.
Heilige Familie. ✢ Holy Family.

# MARY AND THE ANGELS

In sacred texts, angels are often described as messengers from God or as witnesses to the described events. The archangel Gabriel, who told Mary that she would conceive, played a crucial role in the life of the Virgin. But Gabriel was not the only one. The Gospels report that angels, knowing of the birth of Jesus, were the first to tell the shepherds in the hills around Bethlehem.

Images of angels, very rare in the art of the first centuries of Christianity, multiply in the Middle Ages and early Renaissance. Among the first to paint the Virgin and Jesus with angels were the fifteenth-century Florentine artists Fra Filippo Lippi and Sandro Botticelli. Eventually, with beautiful young faces and tall wings, angels overrun religious iconography—at times they are purely ornamental, especially in baroque art. Religious art of the eighteenth and twentieth centuries kept them in sight, tinged with romanticism and sweetness—although the Gospels do not describe the adoration of the infant Jesus by angels, this is represented in a number of holy cards.

Nous avons une mère en Marie
soyons vraiment ses enfants.

We have a mother in Mary. Let us truly be her children.

# THE PIETÀ

---

The term *Pietà* describes representations of Mary grieving the death of her son as she holds his body in her arms; the Latin *Mater dolorosa* also describes this subject. After the Virgin in Majesty and the Virgin of Tenderness, the Virgin of Sorrows is the third major theme of depictions of the life of Mary. When the image includes the other women and other witnesses present at the descent from the Cross, the scene is known as the Lamentation. Painters and sculptors have taken this tragic scene and made it a symbol of the willing sacrifice made by Christ, endured by his mother. The most celebrated is the sculpture of the Pietà by Michelangelo, in the basilica of Saint Peter in Rome.

Even until more recent times, the theme of the "mother of sorrow" has inspired artists. In the nineteenth century, Vincent Van Gogh—otherwise a quite secular painter—rendered this intense drama in several canvases. The simple, naive art of holy cards rarely illustrates the Pietà, staying with secondary themes often linked to matters of doctrine.

O Sainte Mère, imprimez profondément dans mon cœur les plaies de Jésus crucifié !

*O Blessèd Mother, imprint deeply on my heart the wounds of crucified Jesus!*

# THE VIRGIN AND THE LILY

Before becoming the emblem of the kings of France, the lily was the flower of Mary. The Song of Songs in the Old Testament describes a maiden like a lily among thorns. In biblical tradition, the lily is a symbol of choice, a sign that one is chosen by the beloved: Mary was chosen by God to bear his son. The white flower evokes the purity and clarity of divine light; in the pre-Christian cultures of the Near East, the lily represented virginity as well as fertility, two aspects that Mary fulfills. In medieval art, the lily was one of the attributes of the Virgin, as well as being an emblem of Christ, with a symbolic association with royalty.

The language of flowers has retained the notion of purity and virginity for the lily, still one of the flowers of Mary. In the religious iconography of holy cards of the nineteenth and twentieth centuries, romantic images of Mary include extensive use of this flower.

Vierge très pure, vous êtes l'éclat de la lumière éternelle, le miroir sans tache de la majesté de Dieu et l'image de sa bonté.

(Off. de l'Église)

PARIS                3161

GERARD - DESGODETS

*Most pure Virgin, you are the spark of eternal light, the spotless mirror of God's majesty, and the image of His goodness.*

# BLACK MADONNAS

The era of Romanesque art of the Middle Ages has left a number of remarkable Black Virgins. The ones in France represent more than a third of all that have been found. Many of the Black Madonnas draw pilgrimages of uncommon piety, such as those at Rocamadour, Puy-en-Velay, or at Chartres Cathedral in France, and at Montserrat in Spain, Vilnius in Lithuania, and Czestochowa in Poland. Some take the form of painted icons in the Byzantine style, but more often they are statues of modest size. They are generally portrayed as the Virgin in Majesty, seated—even if Mary's sumptuous robes hide her seat—and carved from wood, with rather eastern or Near Eastern features and very elongated hands.

Their sanctuaries are often located at sites of ancient pagan worship. The Black Madonnas are almost always linked to legends telling that they were discovered in dark, dank, hidden places, such as underground, in a cave, in the trunk of a large tree, or in the midst of a grove of trees or thicket—from which they refused to be moved, so that their sanctuaries had to be built on the spot. It was long thought that their dark color came from changes in the wood from which they were carved, but it is now believed that their complexion was an intentional attribute, and that the tradition of the Black Madonnas relates to the veneration of pagan goddesses associated with power and fertility.

# THE SEVEN SORROWS OF MARY

The most painful episodes in the life of Mary have inspired a number of traditional images in art. The Virgin of Sorrows, or *Mater dolorosa*, answers to a variety of other names including Our Lady of Sorrows, Our Lady of Agonies, Our Lady of Mercy, and the Seven Sorrows. Mentioned in the liturgy of the Eastern Orthodox Church from the early Middle Ages, devotion to "the sorrowful mother" did not become widespread until the thirteenth century.

One of the most intense practices honoring the "Seven Sorrows" of the Virgin was initiated by the Servites, members of the Order of Servants of Mary, founded in Italy in 1233 in Florence. This community of contemplative monks centered their devotions on Mary and her course of suffering. They created a special rosary made of seven series of seven beads, which the monks would touch as they recited the seven sorrows, recalling the words of Simeon to Mary in the Temple prophesying the Massacre of the Innocents, the Flight into Egypt, the Disappearance of the Child Jesus in the Temple, her ordeal on the Via Dolorosa as Christ carried the Cross, Mary at the feet of the crucified Christ, Mary holding the body of her son in the Descent from the Cross, and Mary at the tomb of Jesus. In devotional art, these sorrows are often represented by seven daggers or swords piercing Mary's heart. The feast day of Our Lady of Sorrows is the fifteenth of September.

Mater Dolorosa in Monte Calvario venerata
HIEROSOLYMIS

*Proprietas reservata PP. Franciscalium
Custodiae Terrae Sanctae.*

# THE QUEEN OF ARMENIA

The high status of Mary in the liturgy of the Armenian Church is distinctive among the Eastern churches, in that she is referred to as the Queen of Armenia. The major episodes of her life are honored with great festivals preceded by days of fasting. Wednesdays, considered the day of the Annunciation when she received the news of her miraculous pregnancy, are consecrated to her. Legend has it that this veneration goes back to the first century of the Christian era, with the claim that Armenia was evangelized very early by the apostle Bartholomew, the first to bring the message of the cult of the Virgin. If this may seem far-fetched, since Mary was not recognized by the Church as an object of veneration until later, it is true that Armenia embraced Christianity at the beginning of the fourth century.

Gregory the Illuminator, founding father of the Armenian Church, decided that every high altar in the country would be dedicated to the Virgin—a tradition that endures in the Armenian Church to this day. In the tenth century, the Armenian monk Gregory of Narek composed the *Panegyric of the Holy Mother of God*, which cast a mystical light on the figure of Mary. From then on, the Virgin became the mother of the faithful, an image of splendor and wisdom. Rather than promoting the doctrine of the Immaculate Conception adopted by the Roman Catholic Church, the Orthodox credo emphasizes the humanity of the mother of Christ.

Les choses périssables ne sont rien devant Dieu, qu'aucune d'elles ne vous fasse perdre la vue du Seigneur.

*Ephemeral things are naught before God, let them never make you lose sight of the Lord.*

# THE VIRGIN OF THE COPTS

Among Christian communities in Africa, Coptic churches in Egypt and Ethiopia are the oldest. Evangelization began at Alexandria in the first century and extended to Ethiopia by the fourth century. The cult of the Virgin quickly took root among the Copts. Mary is venerated as the mother of Christ, as the universal mother of heaven beside her son, and intercessor between believers and Christ. Passionate devotional literature calls her a golden vase, a fertile earth, an ardent flame, and liturgy gives her a place of honor. Mary is evoked at every stage of the Mass, her name chanted as "lady and queen" at Christ's side.

Coptic worship begins with an offering of incense, when Mary is blessed as the sacred receptacle carrying the incandescent incense that is Christ. Confirming the eminent place held by Mary, the Coptic liturgy includes two long, poetic incantations sung in her honor. Besides the main Christian feast days marking episodes of the life of the Virgin, Coptic Christians observe others, such as the entry of Mary into the Temple. In the Coptic calendar, Christmas is preceded by a month and a half of fasting dedicated to Mary. During this time, every evening is marked by hymns sung to the glory of the Virgin.

O Marie! vous êtes douce aux lèvres de ceux qui vous louent, au cœur de ceux qui vous aiment, au souvenir de ceux qui vous prient.

(St Bernard.)

O Mary! Sweet upon the lips of those who praise you, in the hearts of those who love you, in the memory of those who pray to you.

# MARY AND THE INFIDELS

Intense missionary activity by the Church promoted devotion to Mary. Starting in the thirteenth century, after the Crusades and, later, after the reconquest of Spain from Islamic rule, preaching monks and priests ventured to more faraway lands, in North Africa and Asia. The first Franciscan monk to reach Peking arrived in 1294.

In the era of the early voyages to the Americas of the fifteenth century, efforts to convert non-Christians to the faith corresponded with the spread of colonialism. The most active orders were the Franciscans, Dominicans, and Jesuits—all devoted to the Virgin and committed to propagating this allegiance. In the Americas, they found indigenous cultures that already honored a mother goddess, and identified her with Mary. The Jesuits were envoys of the Counter-Reformation, which intensified devotion to the Virgin; they made the teaching of doctrine their spearhead in their efforts across the world, imbuing their own message with what they learned of local cultures. This helps explain the success of Jesuit missionaries such as Saint Francis Xavier of Spain, one of the original seven Jesuits, who won thousands of converts in Japan in the sixteenth century.

Vierge Marie, priez pour nous
et pour les pauvres petits enfants infidèles.

*(100 j. d'indulgences)*

*Virgin Mary, pray for us, and for the poor infidel children.*

# THE VIRGIN OF GUADALUPE

One of the oldest apparitions of the Virgin Mary occurred in Mexico in 1531. Juan Diego, a fifty-seven-year-old indigenous man who had been converted to the Catholic faith, was on his way to Mass and passed near the hill of Tepeyac, in northwest Mexico. Drawn by the sound of birds singing, he climbed the hill and saw a young woman in a long shining dress. The rocks all around her sparkled, and he saw that rainbows filled the sky. The young woman, who declared to him that she was the Virgin Mary, instructed Juan Diego to build a chapel on that spot.

Juan Diego reported his encounter twice to the priest but met with disbelief. He returned to the hill and confided to the apparition. On the twelfth of December, the Virgin gave him a sign with which to convince the priest: Juan Diego's cloak was miraculously imprinted with her image. No longer doubtful, the priest began construction of a sanctuary, which soon attracted pilgrims. Still today, the miraculous image appears on the cloak as clearly as it did on the first day, and the garment remains in fine condition. Scientific analyses only serve to deepen its mystery. With more than fifteen million visitors, the shrine of Nuestra Señora de Guadalupe on the hill of Tepeyac draws the largest pilgrimage to the Virgin in the world. La Virgen de Guadalupe is the patron saint of Mexico and Latin America.

# THE VIRGIN OF MOUNT CARMEL

Mount Carmel is a mountain ridge that rises above the Mediterranean in Palestine. The Bible tells that the prophet Elijah lived there. In the time of the Crusades in the early twelfth century, a small community of contemplative Christian hermits lived in isolation in the caves on Mount Carmel. They founded the Order of Carmelites, for both monks and nuns, who took vows of poverty, abstinence, silence, and solitude.

In the next century, a man from England named Simon Stock went on a pilgrimage to the Holy Land. He decided to join the community at Mount Carmel, and before long became the father superior. Anxious to nurture the Order, he constantly prayed to the Virgin to place it under her protection. On the sixteenth of July, 1251, she appeared to him and gave him a scapular—an item of cloth to be worn as part of a monastic habit. The Virgin said, "Here is what I grant, to you and to all the children of Carmel. Whosoever dies wearing this habit will be saved." The scapular became the mark of other religious orders, such as the Benedictines and Dominicans. Those who put on this habit commit to a life of devotion to Mary. Among the most esteemed Carmelites are the sixteenth-century mystics Saint Teresa of Ávila and Saint John of the Cross, and the nineteenth-century nun Saint Teresa of Lisieux. Every year on the sixteenth of July, Our Lady of Mount Carmel is honored.

Heilige
Maagd van den
berg Karmel.

F.S.          C.D.V.          Deposé.

# THE BLACK VIRGIN
# OF ROCAMADOUR

The Black Virgin of Rocamadour is a small statue of dark wood found at Rocamadour in the South of France. The faithful attribute miraculous powers to the figure, such as causing church bells to ring upon the rescue of sailors missing at sea. Votive offerings and accounts of intercessions that cover the walls of her chapel reflect her reputation for answering prayers.

According to her legend, devotion to her began with Saint Amadour, a hermit who prayed to the Virgin without cease. The place where he lived, with its austere canyon, encouraged spiritual practice—tradition says that Zacharias, the tax collector who received Jesus into his home, came to finish his days here. A twelfth-century manuscript records many miracles attributed to the Virgin and mentions the major pilgrimage that includes Rocamadour as an essential stop on the route to the sacred site of Santiago de Compostela. A veritable holy city grew little by little at the top of the cliff and Rocamadour became one of the most important centers of medieval Europe, with twenty or so chapels visited by such celebrated figures as Saint Louis, King of France, Queen Blanche of Castile, and King Henry II of England.

ROCAMADOUR. — LA VIERGE MIRACULEUSE

# OUR LADY OF MONTAIGUE

The small Flemish town of Scherpenheuvel hosts the most important pilgrimage in Belgium dedicated to the Virgin; the imposing basilica of Our Lady of Montaigue is proof of its popularity. The basilica owes its existence to stories from the sixteenth century and earlier about a magic oak tree, whose powers had been known since the Middle Ages—in fact, the ancient oak was a site of pagan worship before the Christian era. As the oak grew, it took on the vague form of a cross, and the decision was made to "christen" it by placing a small statue of the Virgin on it. One day a shepherd felt the desire to steal the statue, but the Virgin, irritated, stopped him in his tracks. There he stayed, trapped, until a pilgrim came along and freed him. Convinced that the statue was miraculous, the villagers venerated it, and reports of healings circulated. When famines or epidemics spread, devotion to the Virgin increased tenfold.

A new miracle occurred in 1603, when the statue began to weep tears of blood during the Wars of Religion in the Low Countries. Catholic troops attributed every victory to her, and her reputation grew. In 1607, in the heat of the Counter-Reformation, the Catholic Church decided to build a basilica for her, to encourage devotion and channel the restored fervor of the faithful. The plan and decoration were inspired by the Marian motif of a star with seven points—the cupola alone has 298 of these stars.

ALBERT

ISABELLE

ONZE LIEVE VROUW VAN SCHERPENHEUVEL.

WILLEMS & Cᵉ. BRUXELLES.

DEPOSE.

# THE BLACK VIRGIN OF VILNIUS

Vilnius, in Lithuania, had a large Polish Catholic population until 1945; they venerated a Black Virgin reputed to have miraculous powers of protection and healing. Painted in tempera on oak panels in the manner of Orthodox icons, this Virgin probably dates from the time of the Renaissance. She is sheltered in a small chapel under the arch of one of the ancient entryways to the city, the Aurora Gate, or Gate of Dawn. The rich covering of engraved silver and gold, which gives the Virgin an opulent attire, was added to the image at the end of the seventeenth century and leaves revealed only her face and her hands crossed over her heart. The Virgin stands out against a brilliant sunburst interlaced with twelve stars. She wears two crowns, one above the other, the first to show that she is the Queen of Heaven, the second in homage to the Queen of Poland. The child Jesus is absent.

The thousands of votive offerings surrounding the Black Virgin of Vilnius bear witness to the fervor of countless pilgrims, Catholic and Orthodox, from all over eastern Europe. A miracle of the Black Virgin recorded in 1671 involved a child of two years who fell from a second story and recovered after prayers were made to the icon. The Virgin also worked in defense of Vilnius against her enemies. Also known as Our Lady of the Aurora Gate, her following spread from Lithuania to Poland, the Ukraine, Belarus, and North America.

M. B. Ostrobramska w Wilnie

918

Pd. in Switzerland

# THE MIRACULOUS MEDAL OF CATHERINE LABOURÉ

In April 1830, Catherine Labouré arrived as a novice nun at the motherhouse of the Daughters of Charity, a community founded by Saint Vincent de Paul, situated on the rue du Bac, in Paris. A few days after her arrival, the twenty-five-year-old from Burgundy had three visions in which she saw the heart of the founder, Vincent de Paul. She then received visions of Christ and, finally, three apparitions of the Virgin Mary. The first was on the night of the eighteenth of July. A resplendent child came looking for Catherine in her room and led her to the chapel, where she saw the Virgin seated on the altar. The Virgin foretold troubling times ahead, and ten days later the revolution began that brought Louis Philippe to power as king. This was followed by epidemics that spread through Europe.

A second apparition of the Virgin came on the twenty-seventh of November. The Virgin told Catherine to have a medal made that would commemorate the Immaculate Conception, marked with a letter M, a cross, and the hearts of Jesus and Mary. Anyone who wore such a medal would benefit from its special protection. The third and final vision came in December. In 1832, medals were struck according to the description that Catherine gave, and reports of miracles began to spread. At the time of Catherine's death in 1876, more than a thousand of the miraculous medals had been made.

*O Mary, conceived without sin, pray for us who have recourse to thee.*

# THE LITTLE SHEPHERDS
## OF LA SALETTE

On Saturday, the nineteenth of September, 1846, in a remote village in the French Alps, an extraordinary event occurred. Two children, poor and illiterate—Mélanie Calvat, fourteen, and Maximin Giraud, eleven—were tending their flocks in the high pastures. As they gathered the animals after their rest, a bright light caught their attention. They saw a woman sitting nearby, who called to them. They came closer, and saw that she wore a long white dress and a yellow apron. The woman addressed them, lamenting the loss of faith and indifference of Christians who increasingly neglected to pray. Confronting the incomprehension of the children, she continued in their dialect, predicting ordeals, famine, and epidemics. She told them to pray and to take her message to the world. She then moved to the crest of the slope and floated several feet above the ground. She lingered there a few minutes, suspended in the air in the midst of a brilliant light, then gradually disappeared.

In the following years, disasters throughout Europe matched the predictions. The story of the apparition spread from La Salette, attracting hundreds of pilgrims. Reports of many healings convinced the Church to recognize the authenticity of the apparition of the Virgin of La Salette in 1851.

O.L.V. van Salette    N.D. de la Salette
Bid voor ons.        Priez pour nous.

Steendr. Em. Lombaerts-Van de Velde, Deurne-Antwerpen.

# THE *DEMOISELLE* OF BERNADETTE

In 1858, Lourdes was only a small market town in the Pyrenees in southwestern France, where the Soubirous family lived in poverty. The eldest daughter, Bernadette, was fourteen but could not read or write. On the eleventh of February, the girl went to gather firewood with two friends. She was about to cross a stream when she heard the sound of a strong wind coming from the other side. She looked up and saw a young woman of great beauty silently telling a string of rosary beads. The vision then disappeared. Bernadette's friends had seen nothing. The young woman later appeared to Bernadette again—eighteen times in all, until July.

After Bernadette revealed what she had seen, she was followed by a crowd. When questioned, she described a "young lady" dressed in white with a blue sash, yellow roses at her feet, and a rosary in her hands. The apparition finally told Bernadette to do penance and to drink the water from the spring and bathe in it, and asked that a chapel be built at the spring. On the twenty-fifth of March, the lady identified herself to Bernadette as the Immaculate Conception. The last apparition came on the sixteenth of July. A Church inquest started on the twenty-eighth of July and concluded four years later with a judgment for the reality of the apparitions, in 1862. To this day, of the nearly six thousand accounts of miracles and healings at Lourdes, the Church has recognized only sixty-eight.

Apparition de N.-D. de Lourdes
à Bernadette — 25 Février 1858.

BOUASSE-LEBEL.     2463     PARIS.

# OUR LADY OF GRACE OF BERZÉE

Nothing could foretell that Berzée, a peaceful Walloon village in Belgium of a few hundred souls, would become a center of pilgrimage. In 1909, inside the frame of a simple novena, the parish acquired a painting of Our Lady of Grace. It showed Mary as a sweet face emerging from clouds, wearing a golden star on her shoulder to symbolize her divine maternity. The image had been discovered among ruins in Rome in the sixteenth century; the monk who restored it was said to have put so much passion into his effort that the face in the image inclined toward him and smiled. The Virgin then promised the monk that those who would venerate the image would have their prayers fulfilled. She then fell silent, but her head remained tilted.

The image of Our Lady of Grace left Rome and traveled through Europe, causing miracles in Munich, Vienna, and Prague, before reaching Belgium at the turn of the twentieth century. Once it arrived in Berzée, miracles were so numerous that it was clear that the Virgin herself had decided that the painting should stay there. Reports of miraculous cures spread in Belgium and beyond, and Berzée became the place of the first shrine in Belgium dedicated to Our Lady of Grace. More and more pilgrims came, plastering the walls of the chapel with votive offerings. The second Sunday in July was chosen as the feast day of Our Lady of Grace.

# NOTRE DAME DE GRACE
### VIERGE MIRACULEUSE
### VÉNÉRÉE DANS L'ÉGLISE DE BERZÉE

IMALIT MAREDRET A. P. 47                    MADE IN BELGIUM

# THE VIRGIN OF THE CONGO

Veneration of the Virgin was a part of the evangelization of Africa by Catholic missionaries, and many sanctuaries were dedicated to her. In the Congo, for example, the missionaries who arrived in 1888 founded the congregation of the Immaculate Heart of Mary. The sisters of Our Lady of Namur followed, likewise dedicated to Mary. In 1891, the pope declared the Virgin to be the patroness of the Congo, and made the fifteenth of August, the Day of the Assumption, her feast day there.

NOTRE DAME DU CONGO PPN

Propriété 1906.                    C. van de Vyvere-Petyt, Bruges.

**Notre Dame du Congo,**
vénérée dans l'Eglise des Pères Rédemptoristes à Matadi.

# OUR LADY OF MONTLIGEON

Appointed in 1878 to the little village of La Chapelle-Montligeon in Normandy, Father Buguet lamented the rural exodus that depleted his parish and the loss of faith within his flock. To give the faithful work so that they would stay, he started weaving workshops, without much success. Increasing his efforts, he decided to give attention to the salvation of souls forsaken in Purgatory. With unceasing energy, the good priest promulgated a collection of prayers for the deceased, founding a press—which gave employment to his parishioners—to publish and circulate religious tracts.

Such was his success that by 1895, his work had the attention of every religious association dedicated to souls in Purgatory. The indefatigable country priest of the small Norman parish was even able to finance an imposing sanctuary that he dedicated to Our Lady of Deliverance, where the first Mass was celebrated in 1911. Those praying to the Virgin say, "Take pity on our deceased brethren, intercede for all the departed, and reunite us one day." Father Buguet passed away in 1918.

Notre Dame de Montligeon.

# OUR LADY OF PERPETUAL HELP

In the Middle Ages, an icon of the Virgin and Child was the subject of great veneration on the Greek island of Crete. Known as Our Lady of Perpetual Help, she earned renown for her miracles. In the fifteenth century, Turkish forces invaded the island. Fearing that the icon would fall into the hands of unbelievers, a merchant decided to take her and sail to Italy. Miraculously saved from a storm at sea, he reached Rome and the house of a friend. A few days later, he died, having made a request that the icon be put in a shrine for public veneration. His host ignored his wish and kept the sacred image to himself. The Virgin then appeared several times, insisting that the painting be placed in a church on the Esquiline Hill in Rome, so that all could pray before it. The man failed to understand and continued to keep the painting until, in time, he too fell ill and died. His widow seemed to be no better inclined, and it took the Virgin several more apparitions to win her cause. In 1499, Our Lady of Perpetual Help was placed in the church of Saint Matthew in Rome, where she resumed her miracles.

In the nineteenth century, her sanctuary was destroyed by French troops, and the sacred image disappeared for seventy years. When she was rediscovered, the pope had a new church built in the same place as the plundered shrine. The miracles resumed, and the faithful returned to ask for the Virgin's help.

Notre Dame
de Perpétuel-Secours.

F.S.                    Déposé.

# THE VIRGIN OF DONG LU

Like other Christian missions in China, the one at Dong Lu, near Peking, saw difficult times during the Boxer Rebellion, when nationalists attempted to expel foreigners from China. In 1900, more than ten thousand fighters surrounded the village, where a few hundred Christians lived. It is said that as they prepared their attack, a beautiful woman dressed in white appeared from the clouds. The fighters shot at the apparition, but it did not disappear. Their anger turned to terror when a fiery horseman charged them to drive them away. Despite their great numbers, they fled without harming the Christians.

In thanks to the Virgin, the villagers built a small church dedicated to her, where pilgrims came in honor of Our Lady of China. In 1929, the pope gave recognition to the little church as a Marian shrine. In 1995, an apparition of the Virgin and Child was seen at Dong Lu during a Mass attended by thirty thousand. The next day, an enormous crowd was prevented from reaching the church by government troops. The church was demolished the following year, but an image of Mary and Jesus in Far Eastern dress survived.

Immaculée Conception.

F. Sch. N.    Déposé.

# THE LADY OF MARY ROSE

According to tradition, apparitions of the Virgin Mary occur most often to request that a church be built or to give a message to the faithful. Sometimes the reports start with an individual. In the nineteenth century at Ovalau, one of the islands of Fiji, a missionary had an unexpected visit one day from a local woman. She was dressed in tatters and appeared exhausted. She was not a Christian and did not know the teachings of the Church. Despite the remoteness of her island, she had traveled to see the priest to tell him that a very beautiful woman had appeared to her and told her to take a boat to Ovalau. Astonished and frightened, she told the lady that she did not know the way. The apparition responded, "Do not fear, I will guide you, and when you get there, go into the first dwelling that I show to you. There you will find a white man. Do as he tells you."

The surprised missionary brought the woman to the chapel, where there was an image of the Virgin. The woman exclaimed, "That is the lady I saw on my island!" The priest told her about the Virgin Mary. He then baptized her, giving her the name Mary Rose, and sent her back to her island. Some years later, when missionaries reached that island, they were amazed to find that Mary Rose had converted many of her neighbors.

O MARIA MIDDELARES
ALLER GENADEN. B.V.O.

# THE LADY OF LAKE TITICACA

On the shores of Lake Titicaca in Peru, the people of the village of Puno call the Virgin of Candlemas *Mamita Candelaria*, or "Little Mother of Candlemas"— referring to the feast day of the Purification of the Virgin Mary. Every year for two weeks around the second of February, their patroness is the subject of one of the most important festivals in the country, in which a statue of the Virgin is carried in procession through the streets, presiding over a parade of dancers and musicians.

Many legends are at the center of this Andean tradition, which originates in veneration of the Pachamama, the Earth Mother honored by the indigenous people. Some describe the apparition of a shining woman emerging from the waters of the lake in the midst of flashes of lightning. Others tell of a poor farmer to whom a woman appeared beside a stream, asking if she could wash her son's clothes there. Leaving to look for the landowner, the man returned to find a statue of the Virgin and Child—she was dressed in white, and her son's clothing was still damp. Other accounts tell of the time when villagers carried the statue of the Virgin in procession at night by candlelight when the town was threatened with an attack. Seeing the lights from the heights nearby, the assailants thought they saw an army and fled. After this episode, La Virgen de la Candelaria became the patroness of Puno.

# OUR LADY OF COROMOTO

In Latin America, reverence for the Virgin at first took hold by merging with veneration of an indigenous Earth Mother goddess, called by some the Pachamama. Because of this, the Virgin played a part in smoothing the transition to colonization. In 1651 in Venezuela, the Coromoto people were unwilling to convert. Their *cacique*, or headman, repeatedly saw a splendid woman who carried a child in her arms and who could walk across water. Each time he saw her, this apparition urged him to send his people to receive water on their heads, which she said would allow them to go to heaven. Hearing of this, a Spanish planter arranged for the baptism of many in the Coromoto tribe. But the headman, more willful than his compatriots, refused and fled. One night he saw the apparition again, as beautiful and bright as ever. Exasperated, he jumped up to try to choke her, but she vanished, and the headman was left clutching an image of the Virgin in his hand.

One version of the legend says that on his way to the Spanish plantation after this encounter, the headman was bitten by a poisonous snake. He just managed to reach the place and be baptized, and then he was miraculously cured. His conversion and his subsequent activism encouraged the conversion of many more tribespeople. In Venezuela, Our Lady of Coromoto was declared the country's patroness in 1952.

# THE APPARITION AT KNOCK

The story unfolds in Ireland in the village of Knock, on the twenty-first of August, 1879. On her way home, a girl noticed a strange gleam on the wall of the church. A little later, a young woman named Mary McLoughlin saw the same light. She saw three silhouettes on the wall, which she thought were statues. She returned to the church with a neighbor, and both women saw that the figures moved. Little by little, curious onlookers stopped, perhaps twenty or so. Convinced that this was an apparition, Mary McLoughlin went to find the priest. But he wouldn't come to see, judging that the phenomenon was simply due to a play of light from the windows.

Eventually, fifteen witnesses were questioned, and their statements all agreed. They had seen the Virgin floating about three feet above the ground, dressed in white, crowned with light, her eyes upturned, with a rose at her brow. Beside her, Saint Joseph and Saint John stood over an altar that held a lamb. None of the three spoke, but they remained visible for two hours. In the days following, the story spread and pilgrims arrived in large numbers. Then the first healing occurred—a little girl who had been deaf recovered her hearing. Miracles continued, and the apparition was recognized at an initial inquest, but to this day it has not been made official as a visitation of the Virgin Mary, despite visits to the site by Mother Teresa and Pope John Paul II.

I. BOUASSE J<sup>re</sup> ÉD<sup>r</sup>.  3273  RUE MABILLON, 9, PARIS

REGARDEZ ET FAITES SUIVANT CE MODÉLE.

*Behold, and follow her example.*

# THE VIRGIN OF PEACE
## AT MEDJUGORJE

This occurrence began on the twenty-fourth of June, 1981, in the Catholic village of Medjugorje, near Mostar in former Yugoslavia, in what is now Bosnia-Herzegovina—a region where Catholics, Orthodox, and Muslims have lived as neighbors with great difficulty. On that day, two young girls saw a radiant silhouette on the side of a hill. Frightened, they ran home, but went back that evening with a friend. All three saw the apparition, but this time they saw a woman carrying a child in her arms. A fourth friend came and saw the same thing. They called to a boy who was passing by, and then to another. All saw the lady, but the last ones to arrive panicked and ran off. The next day, the girls and other young people returned. The lady was there, and she asked them to climb up the mountain.

The Virgin continued to appear to the six who had first seen her (four girls and two boys), and eventually was seen by thousands of people—at first every day, then every week, then finally monthly—even to this day. The locations and descriptions of the visions varied, as did her message, but she mostly made appeals for prayer, for love, and for peace. The six young people who first saw her continue to do so. The Catholic Church has not given official recognition to the supernatural character of the apparitions, but Medjugorje has become one of the most-visited Marian sanctuaries in the world.

*Maria onze Koningin*
*Wees gegroet!*

9144        importé d'Italie        DÉPOSE

# THE LITTLE SHEPHERDS OF FÁTIMA

One day in 1915 in Portugal, a girl named Lucia and two friends were watching over their flocks when they saw a pure, shining figure. At Fátima, their village, people made fun of what they described. The next year, Lucia and her two cousins saw the apparition again. It was a transparent young man who told them he was the Angel of Peace. On the thirteenth of May, 1917, the children were again watching over their flocks when a lady appeared and told them to come on the thirteenth day of the next six months. She reappeared on each of these dates. The children were accompanied by some of the curious who had begun to believe them, and who grew in number to nearly four thousand by the thirteenth of July. But only the children could see the Virgin, who said she was Our Lady of the Rosary.

On the thirteenth of October, the day of the last apparition, more than fifty thousand of the faithful recited the rosary with one voice in the rain. The Virgin asked Lucia for a chapel to be built in her honor, and then she rose up into the sky. The rain stopped suddenly and the sun became enormous. During this period, the children saw three new apparitions—of the Holy Family, the Virgin of the Seven Sorrows, and Our Lady of Mount Carmel. A chapel was built in 1919. The pilgrimage to Our Lady of Fátima was officially recognized by the Church in 1930, and attracts more than five million pilgrims to Portugal each year.

Ô MARIE,
HEUREUX LE CŒUR
QUE VOUS CONDUISEZ
À VOTRE DIVIN FILS
DANS L'EUCHARISTIE.

R. P. L. de Bussy.

BOUASSE-LEBEL    2458    PARIS

*Mary, joyful is the heart you lead to your divine Son in the Eucharist.*

# THE VIRGIN OF GLASTONBURY

The destiny of Mary after the death of her son is the subject of several legends. One of the most curious tells of the founding of the abbey of Glastonbury in England. Its founder was said to be Joseph of Arimathea, who gave his tomb for the burial of Christ after the Crucifixion. His legend has him depart for Britain with eleven disciples. There, he built a church dedicated to the Virgin. As proof of her approval, Mary appeared to him, initiating the cult of the Virgin in the British Isles. In truth, the early Christians did not formally venerate the Virgin in the first century, and Glastonbury Abbey was not founded until after the fifth century. In the Middle Ages, an important pilgrimage on the eighth of September honored the birth of the Virgin.

The Glastonbury legend also tells that the Last Supper was held in the house of Joseph of Arimathea, and that he kept the chalice and a little of the blood of Jesus. The sacred vessel—the Holy Grail—became the basis of the story of King Arthur. Some say that the place where Joseph hid the Grail lies somewhere at Glastonbury, under the protection of the Virgin. Henry VIII had the abbey destroyed when he broke with Rome in the sixteenth century. In 1955, a statue of Our Lady of Glastonbury was restored to the site, and was solemnly crowned in 1965.

Salve Regina Mater Misericordiae Salus Populi Romani.

M͞P  Θ͞Y

Sancta Maria Ad Nives Romae

Soc. St Augustin, Lille, Paris, Bruges.                    A.b.47

# THE SMILING STATUE
# OF SAINT THÉRÈSE

Life was not easy for young Thérèse Martin of Lisieux, France. The death of her mother and then her older sister's entry into a Carmelite convent affected her deeply. The girl lost her joy in life, dreaming of nothing besides her catechism and Holy Communion. Her health mysteriously deteriorated, and she suffered from headaches, tremors, abrupt changes of mood, hallucinations, and anguish. Her ailments confounded doctors. On the sixth of April, 1883, her sister was to take her vows as a nun. The following day, Thérèse's symptoms were severe. The girl was delirious and seemed to fall into madness. To ward off this affliction, her family placed a statue of the Virgin next to her bed, but she no longer recognized them and was incoherent.

On the day of Pentecost, her three other sisters kneeled before the statue of the Virgin to beg for help. At this moment, despite her delirium, Thérèse turned to the statue. This was when she saw clearly that the statue smiled at her. Her agitation calmed right away, and the next day she was recovered. When she explained to her Carmelite sister that the statue's smile was the cause of her cure, the whole convent declared it a miracle. Thérèse then embarked on a mystical course that led her to enter into the Carmelite convent at the age of fifteen, under the name of Thérèse of the Child Jesus and the Holy Face.

C'est à Marie
que nous confierons le soin
de nous préparer à la
Communion. Son Bonheur
est de déposer son Fils
dans des cœurs bien purs.

R. P. Eymard.

C. MOREL, EDIT. 1051 RUE St SULPICE, PARIS.

*We turn to Mary to prepare us for communion. It is her joy to lodge her Son in pure hearts.*

# OUR LADY OF AKITA

Agnes Sasagawa was a young Japanese convert to Catholicism. In 1956, she was miraculously cured of her paralysis by the water of Lourdes. One evening in 1973, praying in her convent in Akita, Japan, she noticed a gash in her left hand in the form of a cross. She reported that during the night, the voice of her guardian angel called her to the chapel, which held a statue of Our Lady of All Nations. Although she was deaf, Agnes heard the Virgin urge her to prayer and she remained prostrated in the chapel until early morning. When the other nuns found her, Agnes asked them to look at the hands of the statue, and they saw on the Virgin's right hand a gash the same as hers with a clear trickle of blood. A few days later, the bishop came to see for himself that the two wounds were an exact match and that both were bleeding. In the next three months, Agnes twice heard the statue speak to her again, entreating prayers and repentance and predicting "a fire that would fall from the sky" and "a catastrophe more dreadful than the flood," to rebuke humanity for its waywardness.

From 1975 until 1981, the statue of the Virgin was seen to weep, witnessed by many who reported that her eyes shed a flood of tears. Healings accompanied this phenomenon: Agnes regained her hearing, and a Korean patient recovered from a coma. The Church has recognized the veneration of Our Lady of Akita since 1984.

O ma Mère, mon Espérance
faites que je sois
tout à Jésus.
(S. Alph. de Liguori)

1023.

BOUASSE-JEUNE - PARIS.

O my Mother, my Hope, let me belong wholly to Jesus.

# *LA CONQUISTADORA* OF SANTA FE

The oldest statue of the Virgin Mary in the United States rests in the cathedral of Santa Fe, New Mexico. Carved from wood, it was first brought to Santa Fe in 1625 by Franciscans. Ornately dressed and embellished with a rich head of brown hair arrayed with a set of crowns, she is known as the *Conquistadora*, "Our Lady of the Conquest."

The Virgin became the object of intense devotion after she appeared to a child and miraculously restored her to health from an incurable illness. The girl said the Virgin told her that the people of Santa Fe were to be castigated for their impiety. In 1680, the colony was attacked by neighboring tribes who killed twenty-one friars and expelled the settlers. The statue of the Virgin was rescued from the burning church and taken to Mexico City. Twelve years later, the Spanish decided to retake Santa Fe. The commander in charge, a devotee of the Virgin, attached the statue to his standard and vowed to return it to Santa Fe. As they marched north, the Spaniards pressed the tribes they encountered to acknowledge the love of this universal mother. After four months, the territory was recaptured and more than two thousand souls were caused to convert. When the commander made his triumphal entry into Santa Fe, he dedicated his victory to the Virgin and dubbed her *Conquistadora*. Considered patroness of the town, she was officially dedicated by the Catholic Church in 1960.

DOMINA NOSTRA A SACRO CORDE.
Ora pro nobis.

# MARY IN THE STONE

In Switzerland at Mariastein (which means "Mary in the Stone"), a grotto at the bottom of fifty-four steps holds an especially inspiring statue of the Virgin. Of painted stone, posed on a golden cloud, she smiles sweetly. The venerable history of this simple chapel tells that early in the fifteenth century, a plain wooden statue marked the place where a miracle had happened. According to the story, a small boy in the mountains tending sheep almost had a terrible fall off a cliff, but was carried to the grotto by a beautiful woman. The boy's parents were moved to create a small chapel there, and it soon began to attract pilgrims.

Another legend describes a small girl who fell from a crag, and was caught in midair by the Virgin, who set her down safely in the cave. Then in the sixteenth century, a nobleman in the area was also miraculously saved from a fall into a ravine. In thanks, he made a larger chapel in the grotto, dedicated to Our Lady of Solace. Starting in 1636, a community of Benedictines worked to expand the site.

O Vierge Sainte,
découvrez-nous quelles étaient
vos pensées lorsque vous
contempliez Celui qui venait
de descendre en vous.

(Gerson)

Boumard et Fils
Paris.                                    5216

*O Holy Virgin, reveal to us your thoughts as you contemplated Him who had come down to us through you.*

# THE RECALCITRANTS OF MARCIAC

At the end of the seventeenth century, a plague raged in the region of Gers in southwestern France. A farmer reported that he'd had a vision of the Virgin in the middle of a dazzling light, and that she had told him to build a chapel to Our Lady of the Cross in order to stop the epidemic. But the severity of the Jansenists (who argued for Church reforms for greater moral rigor and asceticism)—and the influence of the early Enlightenment—led to questioning of the proliferation of supernatural phenomena. Few wanted to be seen as superstitious—or fanatic.

The epidemic spread, and ten people died in one day. One evening, the Virgin reappeared to the farmer, but still no one wanted to hear about it. Finally, as the death toll and despair mounted, the people decided to build a shrine. The villagers went in procession to the site of the apparitions to begin to build, and their surprise was real when the epidemic quickly died out. The shrine became an important place of pilgrimage, and today still draws some of the faithful on the Monday after Pentecost.

MARIA . DEIPARA . A . STRATA
ROMAE . COLITUR . IN . TEMPLO . NOMINIS . IESU
A . VATICANO . CAPITULO . A . MDCXXXVIII . AUREO . DIADEMATE . REDIMITA
EOQUE . A . PRAEDONIBUS . PER . VIM . ABREPTO
ITERUM . INSTAURATIS . SOLEMNIBUS . XVIII . KAL . IUL . A . MDCCCLXXXV

Société St. Augustin        A.b. 868.

# OUR LADY OF PROTECTION

In 1490, a farmer was on a hill above the city of Genoa in Italy and saw a lady in a halo of light. She said she was the mother of Christ and asked him to build a chapel for her at that very spot. When the poor man protested that he did not have the means to do so, nor did the land belong to him, she reassured him that she would help him. Going home, he told all of this to his wife, who did not believe him and told him not to speak of it. The next day, the farmer went back to the hill, but he suffered a bad fall that the doctors said he would not survive. Night came, and the Virgin appeared again, repeating her request and telling the man that the fall had been a warning. By morning, he was healed. All the witnesses so marveled at this that the chapel was soon built and dedicated to Our Lady of Protection, according to her request.

In Genoa, custom has it that a salvo of shots be fired to thank the Virgin on the hill for a safe return. Christopher Columbus, the most well known of sailors from Genoa, placed his fleet under the care of Our Lady of Protection. A similar sanctuary dedicated to Our Lady of Protection still exists in Marseilles, France. There, sailors who have been saved from shipwreck have long kept the custom of leaving a votive offering, considering the Virgin to be their protectress.

Mère de Dieu.

# THE WEEPING VIRGIN
# OF MARIAPOCS

The story of the Virgin of Mariapocs in Hungary is one of multiple miracles. In 1696, invading Turkish forces kidnapped the eight-year-old son of Hungarian farmers. After the miraculous rescue of the child, his parents commissioned the painting of an icon of Mary for their church, with Jesus shown holding a tulip in his hand. On the fourth of November of the same year, the painted Virgin began to shed tears of blood during Mass. This happened again three times, the last time on the eighth of December. The Virgin thus manifested her sorrow that Hungary must endure the Turkish invasions.

Devotion to the icon of Mariapocs grew to such an extent that its fame reached the ears of the emperor and empress of Austria, at court in Vienna. They sought out the icon and left only a copy of it in the Hungarian village. But it was in Mariapocs that the Virgin wanted to give proof of her care. From the first to the fifteenth of August of 1715—as well as for an entire month in the year 1905—it was the copy of the icon that shed tears of blood. The phenomena corresponded to times of critical events for Hungary, such as invasion or tensions with Austria. Even during the era of communism, her shrine continued to attract the faithful. The main celebrations in the Virgin's honor are held there on the fifteenth of August, the feast of the Assumption, and the eighth of September, the feast of the Nativity of the Virgin.

Bonne Marie, purifiez nos âmes et nos corps, rendez-nous chastes comme vous.

*Sweet Mary, purify our souls and our hearts, and render us chaste, as thou art.*

# THE VIRGIN AND THE PACHAMAMA IN BOLIVIA

---

The second of February—the feast of the Purification of Mary—is dedicated to the Virgin of Copacabana, patroness of Bolivia. The focus of devotion to her is a modest sixteenth-century statue reputed to have caused great miracles in that era. On the feast day, she was carried in procession, accompanied by ritual dances, songs, and offerings to the Pachamama, the Earth Mother goddess. According to legend, the Virgin of Copacabana miraculously appeared at the same moment in the mountains. Since then, the statue is taken from its shrine in the heights every Ash Wednesday, and the faithful bring her down into the villages to the sound of traditional flutes. The path passes the shrine of the Pachamama, where bottles of water or liquor are left to quench the thirst of the goddess, or cigarettes and ears of corn to thank her for her generosity.

QUE LA SAINTE VIERGE
VOUS COUVRE DE SA SAINTE ET
MATERNELLE PROTECTION
(M<sup>gr</sup> de Ségur.)

BOUASSE-JEUNE                    1317.

*May the Holy Virgin enfold you in her holy maternal protection.*

# THE *PARDONS* IN BRITTANY

The region of Brittany in western France holds a great number of *pardons*, or pilgrimages, held to ask for God's grace for the forgiveness of sins—thus the term *pardon*. A holy statue and relics of the patron saint, or often statues of Mary and her mother Anne, are carried in procession. The biggest concentration of *pardons* occurs on the fifteenth of August, the feast of the Assumption of the Virgin Mary, and on the eighth of September, the feast of the Nativity of the Virgin. A *pardon* might be dedicated to one or the other of the manifestations of the Virgin venerated by the Bretons: Our Lady of Good Help, Our Lady of All Help, and Our Lady of Joy. The route is usually associated with a sacred or miraculous spring, where the people may drink the magical water, a custom inherited from ancient Celtic rites in the region.

Some *pardons* are different, such as the *pardon* of the bikers at Porcaro, in the Morbihan district, initiated in 1979 by a motorcycle-riding abbot who visited Fátima in Portugal and brought back a statue of the Virgin. He wanted her to be venerated as the Madonna of the bikers on Assumption Day. The first year, about forty enthusiasts attended the Mass and benediction. But the *pardon* has since had unexpected success, rallying more than thirty thousand devotees each summer, who come with roaring motorcycles, lining up to be anointed with blessed oil and moving in a humming procession for hours.

Fac me vere tecum flere Crucifixo condolere. Donec ego vixero.

*Grant that I may weep with you in grief for the crucified One, as long as I shall live.*

# THE VIRGIN OF THE GAUCHOS IN ARGENTINA

The story of the most well-known pilgrimage in Argentina goes back to 1630. A convoy traveling with a statue of the Virgin stopped in the village of Luján. In the morning, their animals would not move despite all the efforts of the gauchos. They unloaded the box containing the statue, and the convoy went on its way. Some concluded that the Virgin had wished to stay in Luján. Convinced that this was a miracle, the villagers built her a shrine. In 1681, the humble ceramic statue was given a blue cloak covered with stars. A crown was added, and a halo of shining rays to look like the sun with twelve stars, while a moon was placed beneath her feet. Pilgrims gathered, drawn by her story and accounts of miracles.

Every year, on the last Sunday of September, she attracts the great pilgrimage of the gauchos. More than five thousand assemble in traditional costume and on horseback, with their cattle and gear. Later, on the first weekend of October, thousands of pilgrims leave Buenos Aires on foot to go to prostrate themselves before the statue or to have their babies baptized. The eighth of December, the feast of the Immaculate Conception, is the occasion of a great outpouring of popular fervor, as Our Lady of Luján is also the patroness of immigrants and the poor. Since 1930, she has been the official patroness of Argentina.

La Vierge au Lys

Je vous exalterai, Seigneur, parce que vous m'avez prise sous votre protection.

*(tiré des Psaumes.)*

BOUASSE-LEBEL.　　　1663　　　PARIS.

*The Virgin of the Lily*
*I shall praise thee, Lord, for thou hast taken me under thy protection. (from Psalms)*

# THE VIRGIN OF PUY

The oldest account of an apparition of the Virgin in France comes from the second century, in Velay, in south-central France. According to the legend, a woman named Vila was afflicted for two years with a chronic fever. Unable to bear it anymore, she had herself carried on the night of the tenth of July to Mount Anis, to a prehistoric stone tomb—a *dolmen*—that according to Celtic tradition had magic powers to heal fevers. Nothing happened, and she fell asleep. The Virgin appeared to her and asked her to go to the bishop to convince him to build a chapel there. To reinforce her request, the Virgin miraculously cured Vila, who raced to the bishop to tell him of the apparition and her healing. When the holy man reached the place, he saw for himself another miracle, as the exact location where the healing miracle had happened was now covered in snow, in full summer. A stag rose up and traced the plan of a chapel in the snow. Lacking funds, the bishop nonetheless built a wall of wood to mark the outline of the chapel. A new miracle unfolded the next day, as the wood had sprouted and was covered with blossoms.

Two centuries later, a paralyzed woman was healed on Mount Anis, and had the same vision of Mary requesting her shrine. The cathedral of Our Lady of Puy was finally built in the twelfth century around the magic dolmen, as if to confirm that Christianity had replaced the power of this pagan stone.

Le Seigneur,
ô Marie,

vous a ornée comme le
tabernacle de son choix,

et Jésus Hostie a fait
ses délices

de demeurer en vous.

(P. Eymard)

BOUASSE JEUNE, PARIS    1072

Mary, the Lord hath adorned thee as His chosen tabernacle, and Host Jesus is
pleased to reside in thee.

# *LA MORENETA* OF MONTSERRAT

*La Moreneta*, the "little Moor" in the Catalan language, is a statue of the Virgin that receives intense veneration in Catalonia. She is the object of zealous visits to the abbey on the mountain of Montserrat in northeastern Spain, which started with an apparition of the Virgin in the ninth century. The legend tells that young shepherds tending their flocks in the mountains heard a heavenly song and saw a bright light among the crags. They discovered a cave and inside, the statue of a Black Virgin. They received this apparition more than once, and finally the bishop came to the place to see. But when the bishop tried to move the statue, it was impossible for him to pick it up. He decided to build a small shrine right there. Through the centuries, a number of extraordinary events were attributed to the Virgin of Montserrat, inspiring a popular pilgrimage.

It has since been determined that the statue was carved from poplar wood around the twelfth century, and may not have been black at first. Its veneration mingled little by little with the development of Catalan identity. Local folklore connects the story of *La Moreneta* with the most ancient beliefs, and one tradition tells that the strange rock forms that surround Montserrat are giants that were turned to stone by the Virgin.

# THE VIRGIN OF
# THE ILLUMINATED HILL

With more than five million visitors each year, the Virgin of Czestochowa, in south Poland, attracts one of the largest pilgrimages in the world. Also known as the Virgin of Jasna Gora, the "illuminated hill," the icon was donated by the king of Poland in 1382, when he founded the monastery there. She is a Black Virgin, whose legend tells that her face was painted by the evangelist Luke. During wars in Poland, the walled monastery served as a military center. In 1655, it was attacked by Swedish forces but succeeded in resisting, thanks to help from the Virgin. The story goes that the mark on the Virgin's cheek was made by one of the assailants. The next year, in 1656, the king declared the Virgin Mary the patroness of the country.

The monastery resisted other attacks in the next centuries, from Sweden, Russia, and Austria. The Polish people's veneration for the Virgin of Czestochowa can be measured by the number of votive offerings surrounding the holy icon, which is renowned for its miracles. Hers is the representation of the Virgin that is the most beloved in Poland, and many churches have a copy. During the Solidarity strikes at Gdansk, labor leader (and future statesman) Lech Walesa kept a small reproduction of her on his jacket. The election of the Polish pope, John Paul II, who was extremely devoted to the Virgin, reinforced her popularity in all of Europe.

Oraisons Jaculatoires à Marie.

Sch. N.

Deposé

# THE MIRACULOUS TREE OF HRUSHIV

Apparitions of the Virgin Mary sometimes have reoccurred numerous times in the same place. In the small Ukrainian village of Hrushiv (Grouchevo), Mary appeared one day in a field. The people there were moved to plant a willow and attach an icon of the Virgin. The faithful began to come to pray and leave candles, asking for protection or miracles from Mary. But the tree soon began to wither. A hollow place in the trunk appeared, out of which gushed a miraculous spring. Its water was a cure for all kinds of maladies, drawing more and more pilgrims.

In May of 1914, the Virgin appeared there again, to more than twenty people. She predicted terrible events to come that would last more than eighty years. She predicted that Christians would be persecuted and that there would be three wars, but that in the end, the Ukraine would be free. Much later, on the twenty-sixth of April, 1987, one year to the day after the nuclear catastrophe at Chernobyl, a little girl from Hrushiv saw the silhouette of a woman walking on the balcony of the chapel. The apparition showed herself each day at the same time. Many people reported seeing the Virgin of Hrushiv and hearing her confirm her help to the Ukrainian people and her promise that they would be free.

N. D. Auxiliatrice

663

# THE MAGIC CANDLE OF THE VIRGIN

In 1105, a terrible epidemic of epilepsy struck the region of Artois in northwestern France, causing convulsions, hallucinations, and gangrene. The bishop of Arras prayed to the Virgin to bring relief. Mary then appeared to two *trouvères* (poets) who detested each other. She commanded them to go to Arras, where they would receive a church candle. They then had to reconcile and light their candle in the presence of the bishop. They were to let the candle wax drip into containers full of water and give the water to those who were ill. Those who had faith would be cured, and the rest would die.

The two enemies did as they were told. In the cathedral of Arras, they saw the Virgin come down from the vaulted ceiling in a flood of light, carrying the miraculous candle. When they took the candle, the Virgin disappeared. The poets gave the water for the ill to drink and anointed their sores with the liquid. That same day, the 144 dying people in the cathedral were cured. The taper was given the name of Saint Candle, and its drips were used to make a great quantity of other holy candles, which were distributed in the churches of Artois. In the thirteenth century, the brotherhood of minstrels and bourgeois of Arras organized a devotional group for the veneration of the miraculous candle.

O MARIE, FAITES QUE JÉSUS REPOSE TOUJOURS
DANS MON CŒUR ET QUE JE REPOSE TOUJOURS
DANS LE CŒUR DE JÉSUS.

(St Al. de Liguori)

*O Mary, let Jesus always reside in my heart, and let me always reside in the heart
of Jesus.*

# THE MOTHER OF GOOD HEALTH
## OF VELANKANNI

The first apparition of the Virgin Mary in India came about in the sixteenth century at Velankanni, a village in the province of Madras. Tradition says that a young shepherd on his way to bring milk to his mother, drowsing at the side of the road, dreamt that he saw a beautiful lady who asked for some milk for her son. He generously gave her some right away, all the while dreading his mother's reprimands. But when he arrived safely home, he found that his jar was full again. Another apparition of the Virgin came to a disabled child who offered a drink to the young Jesus and was miraculously healed.

A third apparition rescued Portuguese sailors about to drown in the Bay of Bengal. A chapel with a statue of the Virgin was built there and soon attracted devotees, Hindu as well as Catholic, who witnessed so many miracles that the Virgin was called the Mother of Good Health. Every year on the Marian festival of the eighth of September, millions of pilgrims come to Velankanni to honor the Virgin.

# L'ENFANT DE MARIE

*O ma Souveraine! O ma Mère! Souvenez-vous*
*que je vous appartiens. Gardez-moi, défendez-moi*
*comme votre bien et votre propriété.*

40 jours d'Ind.

MAISON BOUASSE-LEBEL — Lecène & Cie PARIS     5545     MADE IN FRANCE

*Child of Mary*
*O my Queen! O my Mother! Remember that I am yours. Keep me, defend me as*
*your belonging and your property.*

# THE APPARITION AT ZEITOUN

In Zeitoun on the outskirts of Cairo, a rich Copt who planned to build a house had a vision of the Virgin, who asked him to build a chapel there instead. She told him that she had passed that way with Joseph and Jesus at the time of the Flight into Egypt. In 1924, the man fulfilled her request and constructed a beautiful church with five domes. Much later, in 1968, workers employed at a mechanic's shop across the street saw a woman dressed in white atop the main dome of the church. Thinking that she was someone about to commit suicide, perhaps a nun, the workers called out to her and summoned the police. The priest and other witnesses also saw her and understood that she was an apparition.

The Virgin reappeared several times in the following days, to Muslims as well as to Christians. Sometimes she was accompanied by the child Jesus, sometimes by Joseph, or by both. Always silent, she remained visible for long moments, her appearances preceded by lightning flashes and flights of white birds. The apparitions continued several times each week for fourteen months, sometimes attracting fifty thousand witnesses. Healings occurred and photographs were even taken to document the phenomena. In 1969, the Coptic pope established the feast of the Transfiguration of the Virgin, celebrated at Zeitoun on the second of April.

*Riches and honor are with me, to endow those who love me.* PROVERBS 8:18

# THE STATUE AT BALLINSPITTLE

In 1954, several grottos resembling the one at Lourdes were made in Ireland. Strangely, in 1985, reports arose of visions of the Virgin at more than thirty of these. Most often, a movement of the statue of the Virgin caught the attention of visitors. Each time, the Virgin gave a message urging prayer and warning of the end of the world unless humankind came to God.

In County Cork, Cathy O'Mahony and her daughters were among the witnesses to these visions when they went to the grotto at Ballinspittle to pray. On the way to the grotto, a statue of the Virgin with a halo of electric lights stands in the rocky landscape. As she approached, Cathy thought that the statue could be seen to breathe and move. The news spread quickly and crowds gathered in an atmosphere of intense fervor. Hundreds of thousands of pilgrims came from all over the country to pray at the foot of the statue. Over a third of them said that they saw the Virgin move, and some said that they saw her rise off the ground. Collective hallucination or miracle, the Irish bishops have declined to say, reluctant to fuel the overwhelming fervor.

MARIE,
TABERNACLE
VIVANT,
DONNEZ-NOUS TOUJOURS
VOTRE HOSTIE DIVINE:
JÉSUS!

P. Eymard.

BOUASSE-LEBEL.     2467     PARIS.

*Mary, living Tabernacle, may you ever grant us your Divine Host, Jesus!*

# OUR LADY OF BLISS

There were once three very devout brothers from the town of Laon, in the north of France. They went on a Crusade, but were captured by Muslims and taken to the grand sultan in Egypt. The sultan wanted to convert them to Islam, and asked his daughter for help. To convince the brothers, the young lady asked them to talk about their own faith. She seemed to be very interested to hear about the life of the Virgin Mary, so the eldest brother offered to make her a statue, but he did not know how to carve. That night, when the three prisoners were sleeping, they were awakened by a sound like an angel singing. The Virgin herself had placed a statue in their cell, a figure so radiant and that filled them with such joy that they named her Our Lady of Bliss.

The next day, the brothers offered the statue of the Virgin to the sultan's daughter, who took it to her chamber. That night, it was to her that the Virgin appeared in a dream, telling her to free the brothers and to become a Christian. The young lady freed the prisoners and, taking the statue with her, followed them to France, where she had herself baptized and took the name of Mary. One of the brothers had a chapel built for the miraculous statue. The pilgrimage to Notre-Dame de Liesse, near Soissons in Picardy, became renowned for healings, and was one of the most highly attended in France until the French Revolution.

O Marie,
apprenez-nous à trouver
comme vous tous les mystères
et toutes les grâces en
l'Eucharistie.

(P. Eymard)

O Mary, teach us to find, as you have, all the mysteries and grace of the Eucharist.

# PRINCIPAL FEAST DAYS OF THE VIRGIN MARY

**1 January** Feast of Holy Mary, Mother of God

**2 February** Feast of the Presentation of Jesus in the Temple, or Feast of the Purification of Mary (The Festival of Lights)

**11 February** Feast of Our Lady of Lourdes

**25 March** Feast of the Annunciation

**2 April** Feast of the Transfiguration of the Virgin

**31 May** Feast of the Visitation

**Second Sunday, July** Feast of Our Lady of Grace

**16 July** Feast of Our Lady of Mount Carmel

**5 August** Feast of the Dedication of the Basilica of Santa Maria Maggiore, Rome

**15 August** Feast of the Assumption

**22 August** Feast of the Queen of Heaven and Feast of the Immaculate Heart of Mary

**8 September** Feast of the Nativity of the Virgin Mary

**15 September** Feast of Our Lady of Sorrows

**7 October** Feast of Our Lady of the Rosary

**21 November** Feast of the Presentation of the Virgin Mary

**8 December** Feast of the Immaculate Conception; Feast of the Nativity of Mary

**Sunday following Christmas** Feast of the Holy Family

Regina liliorum

BOUASSE JEUNE      1285.      PARIS.

# OTHER TITLES IN THE SERIES

***The Little Book of Angels.*** Nicole Masson. Translated by Elizabeth Bell.

***The Little Book of Saints.*** Christine Barrely, Saskia Leblon, Laure Péraudin, Stéphane Trieulet. Translated by Elizabeth Bell.

VENEZ À MOI!

Je suis la Mère du Saint Amour,
de la Crainte, de la Science,
et de la Sainte Espérance.

(Eccl. 24.)

BOUASSE-LEBEL.        1656.        PARIS.

*Come to me! I am the mother of fair love, and fear, and knowledge, and holy hope.* ECCLESIASTICUS 24:18

O Marie, nous nous
consacrons à vous
pour toujours

M.H.                                    3177